I0417987

Misquoted

*Things we think are in the Bible,
but are not*

Russell Muilenburg

DEDICATION

For Beth. You inspire me to communicate well.

CONTENTS

Introduction
CHRISTIANISMS

From the French

Back in the days of printing presses, the iron plate which was etched with the words, phrases, or images to be printed was known as a *stereotype*. Whenever this plate pressed down to reproduce another page, it would make a loud noise which, for French printers, sounded a lot like their word for "click." That word is "cliché."

Thus, cliché came to mean a saying that gets repeated often. Or, we might say, a stereotypically simplistic and tired phrase.

Generally speaking, clichés are statements which were striking and thought-provoking when first coined; but which have become unoriginal and overused. Popularity makes them seem trite. Often, the original meaning of the phrase is lost and the statement comes to stand for a whole range of barely understood ideas.

As Christians, we have a tendency to adopt sayings that reduce deep truths about God and our world to clichés. I call them "Christianisms." Sometimes they are referred to as "Christianese." There are dozens of them. Pithy, memorable sayings that Christian people repeat over and over again that look good on fridge magnets and tasteful t-shirts.

My contention is that most of these phrases are not that helpful and—worse than that—many are not even true. This book is about some of these clichés.

Filling the Cracks in our Conversations

I think of the phrases covered in this book as verbal filler. These sayings are the sort of things that Christians use to fill in the cracks in our conversations.

Imagine you are talking to a friend. That friend is sharing something heavy that has recently happened: a parent diagnosed with an illness, a child who has been in trouble at school, a job situation that has turned ugly.

It's an emotional situation. There's a long pause,
a crack in the conversation.

You want to offer comfort and encouragement. Above all, you want to bolster this person's faith in God. So you reach for the trowel and you fill the crack with some verbal spackling:

- "God won't give you more than you can handle."
- "Everything happens for a reason."
- "You've gotta just let go and let God."

These are Christian clichés. They are statements we make without really thinking them through. They are so familiar to us that we accept them as unquestioned truth. We hear them so often that we assume they are helpful.

But this kind of verbal filler rarely withstands careful consideration. Your friend might feel you are being truly caring in the moment—and you are trying!—but if they take time to reflect on what you have said, they are going to find there isn't much comfort to be had there.

Singing Songs to a Heavy Heart

Proverbs 25:20 says: "Like one who takes away a garment on a cold day, or like vinegar poured on a wound, is one who sings songs to a heavy heart."

If it's cold outside, and you come by and take away my coat, that's not gonna help me. Likewise, if I have an open sore, and you come by and throw vinegar on there, that's gonna hurt me worse.

In the same way, if I am stricken by grief and you come to me with empty platitudes and cheap clichés, that's just not helpful. It's like asking me to go to an upbeat concert when what I really want to do is sit at home and eat ice cream.

We live in the day of the sound bite, the meme, and the Tweet. We love to capture that perfect line that sums up complicated issues in a way that is memorable and quotable. That's one of the reasons these sayings have endured. They seem to express profound thoughts about God and life with an economy of words.

But when we reduce the great mysteries of evil and suffering to a slogan that will fit on a bumper sticker, it's inadequate. It's patching up a hole in the wall with bubble gum and masking tape. It ignores the depth of the pain by going for a pat answer. When we resort to clichés like those covered in this book, we are just as likely to convey an attitude of un-concern as we are to convey truly helpful care. That's singing songs to a heavy heart.

What your friend in that tough situation needs is not a carefully crafted catchphrase, but a shoulder to lean on and a listening ear.

Be Like the Bereans

I would like all of us to stop using the phrases in this book because they are not that helpful. But I have a deeper reason: they're not Biblical either.

The subtitle of this book is "Things we think are in the Bible, but are not." Most of the sayings I chose to examine get quoted so frequently by believers, and with such certainty, that it seems like we are citing a Bible text. If I can help us realize that not everything we repeat like a Bible verse is an actual Bible verse, that will be a win.

My beef with these sayings, however, is not just that the exact wording is not found in the pages of Scripture. There are plenty of true statements that do not come directly from the Bible. Every week I prepare a sermon which I try to summarize in one or two key phrases. Those phrases are usually not direct quotes from the Bible, but I hope they capture Biblical ideas. A phrase does not need to be a quote from the Bible in order to be true.

When I say that the clichés in this book are not Biblical, what I mean is that the ideas they convey are not in keeping with Biblical teaching. My beef with these clichés is that they give misleading or incomplete pictures of God and our relationship with Him.

In Acts 17, Paul's missionary journeys led him to the Greek city of Berea. It's a small part of Paul's story, covering just a few verses. And nothing terribly noteworthy appears to have happened in Berea. But in recounting his brief stay, the narrator of Acts (Luke) makes this praiseworthy observation of the Bereans: "Now the Berean Jews were of more noble character than those in Thessalonica, for they received the message with great eagerness and examined the Scriptures every day to see if what Paul said was true" (Acts 17:11).

The Bereans were eager listeners, but they were also critical listeners. They didn't just accept the things Paul said because he was Paul. They weren't roped in by the power of his presentation or the cleverness of his phrasing. Instead, they went back to the Scriptures to see if Paul's teaching was in accordance with what God had already revealed about Himself.

Ultimately, that's what I hope this book will help us all to do. The sayings covered in this book have been repeated so often in the English-speaking world of Christianity, and with such confidence, that we accept them uncritically. They are conventional wisdom. Truisms. We hear them so often we don't even think to question them.

But we must question them. We must examine the Scriptures to see if what has been accepted as conventional wisdom is true.

It's not just that they are misquotes of things that sound vaguely Biblical, they can also be dangerous. Built on false assumptions and misunderstandings about God, these sayings, and the beliefs that underpin them, can lead to disillusionment and frustration when they fail to hold true. A wall that is patched with inferior material is going to crumble. As Jesus said in the parable of the two builders, a house built on sand will one day fall with a crash (see Matthew 7:24–27).

I hope this book will help us all to reconsider some of the clichés and pat answers we might have been prone to accept unblinkingly in the past. I also hope this book will give us the tools to be like the Bereans in examining Scripture to see if what we are being told is true. Not just in the phrases looked at in this book, but in the vast array of other Christianisms that are bound to come our way.

Gameplan

Please understand, my goal is not to make anyone feel bad if you have used these phrases. I've said all these phrases on multiple occasions, even after beginning work on this project. They are such a part of our Christian world that I don't know if they will ever go away altogether. But I do want us to think more carefully about the things we say and hear.

My plan, then, with each statement is to ask a form of the following three questions:

1. First, I want us to inquire: **Is there any Biblical truth?**

Something doesn't become a cliché unless it is based on some truth. Surely there is a reason each of these statements has become so popular among Christians. With each phrase, then, I'll give my best-faith effort to find the Biblical teaching that supports the idea.

2. Second, I want us to ask: **Where does the statement go wrong?**

This is where we need to think critically. Just because these statements get used so often doesn't mean they are entirely true. In fact, with each Christianism I've picked out for us to look at, there's something that makes it more of a cheap cliché than a timeless truth. And I want us to look carefully at what that might be, in order to keep us from saying things to one another that are really not that helpful.

3. And then, third, with each statement I want us to ask: **Is there better news in the gospel?**

If these are not Biblical ideas, we need to look to see what the Bible really does say. Each of these statements is an attempt to convey good news, but, in each case, I believe the gospel of Jesus Christ gives even better news.

And that, of course, is where we want to base our faith.

What's In It for You?

I want you to think Biblically about the beliefs, slogans, and popular ideas that we often tend to receive passively and uncritically. More than that, I want you to be able to think Biblically, period.

This book will help you apply a Biblical framework to all the information you receive, not just tired clichés. By applying these three questions to the phrases covered in the following chapters, this book will model for you how to think critically whenever you hear declarative statements that sound a little too precious. Here are the three questions we can ask of each message we receive:

- What's true about this?
- Where does it get off track?
- Is there better news in the gospel?

If we make it a habit to continually ask those questions, it will serve us well.

It's upon the timeless truths of Jesus, and not the cheap clichés of trendy religion, that we want to build our lives. This book will help you do so.

66

— 1 —

GOD HELPS THOSE WHO HELP THEMSELVES

Jaywalking

Ponder this: the most popular Bible verse in America is not even a Bible verse!

When Jay Leno hosted *The Tonight Show* he had a recurring comedy gag called "Jaywalking." The idea was that he would go out on the street and ask random people really basic questions. For example, he would show people a picture of the current vice-president and ask them to identify that person. The comedy came in how often people would get the simplest questions wrong.

One night, the premise of Jaywalking was to ask people to name one of the 10 Commandments. Overwhelmingly, the most popular response was, "God helps those who help themselves." This is not one of the 10 Commandments. It's not even a command and—you guessed it—it is most definitely not in the Bible.

Christian pollster George Barna has often used this phrase to measure Biblical literacy in America. I don't want to overwhelm you with numbers, but he has found that about 75% of Americans agree strongly or agree somewhat that the Bible teaches that God helps those who help themselves. Among Christians, about 68% agree that the phrase is Biblical. In another poll, the phrase came in first as the most widely known Bible verse.[1]

Why is this cliché so persistently popular?

The Value of Hard Work

Let's start by looking for Biblical truth in this statement. Even though the exact phrasing is not in the Bible, is the idea at least found there?

And the answer is yes, sort of. If you see the phrase as promoting a form of personal responsibility, then it is something the Bible teaches.

Consider 2 Thessalonians 3:10–12:

> For even when we were with you, we gave you this rule: "The one who is unwilling to work shall not eat."
>
> We hear that some among you are idle and disruptive. They are not busy; they are busybodies. Such people we command and urge in the Lord Jesus Christ to settle down and earn the food they eat.

One of the themes of Paul's letters to the Thessalonians is the return of Jesus. Paul had encouraged the Thessalonians to put their faith in Jesus, and also to trust that Jesus could return at any time. As a result, however, some had taken the extreme step of quitting their jobs and spending all of their money in the assumption that God would provide them with all they needed.

When Paul hears about this, he is quick to nip it in the bud. Trusting in Jesus does not mean you stop taking responsibility for yourself. Believing that Jesus will take care of you does not mean you simply sit on the couch all day and wait for your food to miraculously appear. You can pray for your daily bread, but then you should also go out and earn it. Proverbs 10:4 says much the same thing: "Lazy hands make for poverty, but diligent hands bring wealth."

The Bible has a pretty strong doctrine of personal responsibility. Benedictine monks use a Latin phrase, *ora et labora*, which means "pray and work."

Our faith is meant to move us to action. Even as we pray, we are expected to go to work. In that sense, "God helps those who help themselves" is a Biblical idea.

If you've ever prayed for God to make a situation different, and then decided to go to work to try to make some changes, you have captured the essence of this phrase. You are praying and working if you are:

- The person who prays for better health and then begins an exercise program.
- The person who asks God for a better job and then starts mailing out resumes and working the phones.
- The person who wants help to stop swearing and then starts putting a dollar in the swear jar with every bad word.
- The person who prays for a neighbor to come to know Jesus and then sets about developing a friendship with that neighbor.

These are all examples of praying and working. These are ways that the phrase "God helps those who help themselves" can be Biblical and helpful.

The phrase itself, however, has an unbiblical origin. Scholars believe, in fact, that the idea first appeared about 400 years before Paul wrote his letter to the Thessalonians. The Greek playwright Sophocles wrote, "No good e'er comes of leisure purposeless; And heaven ne'er helps the men who will not act."

At about the same time that Paul was alive, a collection of stories known as Aesop's fables was being put together. One was called "Hercules and the Waggoner."

It told the story of a man whose wagon was stuck in the mud along the side of the road. The more the man's horses strained against the traces, the deeper his wagon sunk. So he kneeled down and prayed for Hercules to come along and help him, at which point Hercules appeared and said something along the lines of, "Put your shoulder to the wheel, man, and urge on your horses. Do you think you can move the wagon by simply looking at it and whining about it? Hercules will not help unless you make some effort to help yourself."

In English, the phrase was probably made most famous by Benjamin Franklin, who included it in his *Poor Richard's Almanac* in 1736. Ever since, "God helps those who help themselves" has been considered a very American way of looking at things. It praises the value of hard work and cautions us against laziness.

Bending the Rules to Get Ahead

But there are also ways this statement can be harmful. Now we need to ask, where does it go wrong?

For one thing, this phrase can sometimes be used as an excuse for taking ethical shortcuts.

Imagine two teenagers working the counter at their local ice cream shop when the manager steps out to visit with a customer. Since no one is looking, one of the teens hits "no sale" on the cash register and slips a couple of $20s into his pocket. When his co-worker whispers, "Hey, what are you doing!?" the teen replies, "Relax, nobody will miss it. Besides, 'God helps those who help themselves.'"

Or, again, imagine a start-up company hoping to land an infusion of funds from an angel investor. When the venture capitalist shows uncertainty regarding the new company's business potential, the start-up's founder convinces a friend to call in pretending to represent a large corporation and hinting about possible future business deals with the start-up. When the friend expresses hesitation at such dishonesty, the start-up guy says, "Relax, this is how business gets done. Besides, 'God helps those who help themselves.'"

Theft and fraud are ways to help oneself, but it is hard to make the case that God approves of such behavior. You can backstab a co-worker in order to get a promotion. You can trip an opponent on the basketball court when the referee's back is turned. You can get creative with your bookkeeping at tax time. All of those behaviors and more may result in tangible rewards and earthly success, but that doesn't mean that God is helping or blessing you for those behaviors.

In fact, the Bible is quite clear that God abhors those who use dishonest means to get ahead (Proverbs 11:1). The prophet Micah called out the wicked businessmen of his day who used undersized measuring devices when selling flour and false weights on their scales (Micah 6:10–11). His message to them on God's behalf:

> You will eat but not be satisfied;
>   your stomach will still be empty.
> You will store up but save nothing,
>   because what you save I will give to the sword.
> (Micah 6:14)

In other words, you might feel like your ethical shortcuts are getting you ahead, but don't make the mistake of thinking that God is blessing you or helping you. Quite the contrary, a time is coming when justice will be done.

Saying that God helps those who help themselves is not a justification for immoral behavior.

Callous Hearts

While it's pretty easy to see where the ethical shortcut use of this cliché goes wrong, another problem with the way this phrase is often used is a bit more insidious. Sometimes this phrase can be used as a way of getting out of our call to love our neighbors. In particular, this phrase will often be used to weaken our responsibility to the poor.

This is the thinking that leads motorists to yell "get a job!" when driving past panhandlers at an intersection, or the mindset that leads a church to cut down on benevolent giving when the budget gets tight. Too often I have heard people argue against making donations to help the poor and needy because those people should be helping themselves.

In Scripture, however, God consistently calls us to help those who cannot help themselves. In fact, in the material sense, it seems that God's preferred way to help those who cannot help themselves is through the compassion, generosity, and creativity of His people.

Consider Deuteronomy 15:7–8:

> If anyone is poor among your fellow Israelites in any of the towns of the land the LORD your God is giving you, do not be hardhearted or tightfisted toward them. Rather, be openhanded and freely lend them whatever they need.

Do not be tightfisted. Scripture does not ask us to judge why the poor are in the situations they are in. It doesn't ask us to make judgments about whether they are able-bodied enough to get out of poverty on their own. It simply says, "be openhanded and freely lend them whatever they need."

James 1:27 says this: "Religion that God our Father accepts as pure and faultless is this: to look after orphans and widows in their distress and to keep oneself from being polluted by the world."

The use of the word "religion" here might throw you off. A lot of Christians want to emphasize that Christianity is more about a relationship with Jesus than it is about the performance-based hoop-jumping of a lot of religious experience. James would want that too.

James does not want us merely paying lip-service to God, performing superficial rituals without being authentically changed. Bad religion, worthless religion, is the kind of religion which allows us to hide behind a veneer of pious actions.

But true religion, the kind of religious observance that the Father accepts as pure and faultless, is authentic. It gives evidence that it is real.

And one of the main ways we show evidence of a genuine relationship with Jesus is by looking after widows and orphans. That is to say, we demonstrate that our faith is real when we help those who are not in a position to help themselves.

When Jesus tells a story to illustrate what it means to love our neighbors, He tells of a priest and a Levite who crossed to the other side of the road to avoid interacting with a man who had been beaten by bandits. I can imagine them muttering to themselves, "God helps those who help themselves," as they hurried on their way.

But the Good Samaritan did not. He did not ask questions about what the man deserved or had earned. He did not even worry about the ethnic divisions that made interaction with him taboo. He simply jumped in and helped.

15

And we know which one was commended by Jesus. (See Luke 10:25–37.) Loving our neighbor is commanded in Scripture without condition.

The Better News of Grace

If the phrase "God helps those who help themselves" is not found in the Bible, is there something in Scripture that gives better news? Our third question: Is there better news in the gospel?

I would say "Yes!" Very much, "Yes."

In fact, probably the worst thing about this phrase is that it runs counter to the Bible's most important message, and that is God's care and provision for us.

Rather than "God helps those who help themselves," I would argue the central message of the Bible is that God loves to help those who cannot help themselves. It is at our point of greatest need that God loves to enter in and help. Consider Psalm 10:14, 17–18:

> But you, God, see the trouble of the afflicted;
>> you consider their grief and take it in hand.
> The victims commit themselves to you;
>> you are the helper of the fatherless.
>> ...
> You, Lord, hear the desire of the afflicted;
>> you encourage them, and you listen to their cry,
> defending the fatherless and the oppressed,
>> so that mere earthly mortals
>> will never again strike terror.

Look at those phrases: "Victims commit themselves to you." "You are the helper of the fatherless." In other words, God helps those who are helpless. The orphan, the one with no resources.

Verse 17 says, "You, LORD, hear the desire of the afflicted, you encourage them, and you listen to their cry." God is not waiting around for us to push our wagon out of the mud. He's waiting for the cry of those who realize they can't fix things on their own.

Adam Hamilton writes:

> God is the God of the hopeless cause, the God who loves sinners, the God who walks with us through the darkest valleys. He is the God who brings light into our darkness and helps us find peace amid our times of anxiety and despair. God rescues, redeems, and forgives. We receive blessings from God even though we cannot earn them and don't deserve them. Even when we have made a mess of things and can't fix them, God extends mercy to us. There's a word for God's mercy toward those who cannot help them-selves. We call it grace.[2]

The danger of the phrase "God helps those who help themselves" is that it can turn our salvation into a salvation of works. It gives the impression that we must earn our way to heaven. That only those who prove themselves good enough will be accepted by God. And the problem with that is that none of us will ever prove ourselves good enough. None of us can earn our way to salvation.

Paul addresses the idea of earning salvation through works in the book of Romans. Talking about Abraham, he examines the idea of whether it was Abraham's good works or his faith that brought him into favor with God. Paul quotes Genesis 15, which says that "Abraham believed God, and it was credited to him as righteous-ness" (Romans 4:3).

Then he writes: "Now to the one who works, wages are not credited as a gift but as an obligation. However, to the one who does not work but trusts God who justifies the ungodly, their faith is credited as righteousness" (Romans 4:4–5).

In other words, the Bible would not say that Abraham was credited with righteousness if it was something he earned. If God was rewarding Abraham because Abraham first helped himself, then it wouldn't be salvation by grace, it would be salvation by works. And that would mean that God was waiting around for all of us to make ourselves good enough for His love.

But that's not how it works. That's not the good news of the gospel. In the next chapter of Romans, Paul puts it like this:

> You see, at just the right time, when we were still powerless, Christ died for the ungodly. Very rarely will anyone die for a righteous person, though for a good person someone might possibly dare to die. But God demonstrates his own love for us in this: While we were still sinners, Christ died for us. (Romans 5:6–8)

Do you hear that? "When we were still powerless." Christ didn't wait for us to help ourselves. We were powerless to do so. We were still lost in our sins. But that didn't stop God. He sent Christ into the world and Christ died for us while we were still unlovely.

The message of the secular world might be that God helps those who help themselves. In a competitive, individualistic culture, it is everybody for themselves and you better get what you can while you can.

But the better news of the gospel is that God helps those who cannot help themselves. The better news of the gospel is grace.

And it is essential for all of us to recognize how much we need God's grace in our lives. It is essential for us to recognize that in the face of our sin and our unrighteousness, we are powerless to help ourselves.

So what about you? Are you going to tell God to stand aside while you figure things out for yourself? Are you going to try to earn your standing with God through a little self-determination and elbow grease?

Or are you going to admit that you are a sinner in desperate need of grace? Are you going to acknowledge that you are helpless to do anything about your plight, and ask Jesus to come to your rescue?

God helps those who cannot help themselves. That's the good news of the Bible. That's the best news of all.

For further study, see the Discussion Guide for
Chapter 1 on page 126.

− 2 −

LET GO AND LET GOD

Jesus, Take the Wheel

Before reading the following story, it is good to know that no one was seriously injured.

An Ohio woman caused an impressive amount of carnage after running a red light at over 100 mph and crashing through multiple cars, a utility pole and a house. The reason for the crash is perhaps even wilder as the driver admits to running the light with her kid in the car on purpose to "test her faith with God."

On June 15, police in Beachwood, Ohio, responded to the scene of the incredible crash, reports 19 News Cleveland. The driver had her 11-year-old kid in the car and thankfully there were no major injuries to her, the kid, the driver of the other car or occupants of the house. Traffic camera videos captured her Ford Taurus taking the nose off of one car in an intersection before crashing in the next.

The police investigation into the crash took a weird turn when the woman admitted to police that she intentionally sped down the road and through the intersections at about 120 mph. From KTLA 5:

> The woman told police that she intentionally drove at the high speed and through the red light to "test her faith with God," according to the report.
>
> She told police she's been going through some "trials and tribulations" and was recently fired from her job.
>
> The woman said she "let go and let God take the wheel," the police report said, adding that she believed she did the right thing.

Weirdly, crashes where people just let go of the wheel happen more often than you'd probably expect. In 2020, a Pennsylvania woman rammed a Kia Optima into a car as a "test of faith," reports the Mercury News. In 2018, a Tennessee man rolled his truck five times after letting go of the wheel, reports [the] Miami Herald.[3]

It's a strange story, and one that we probably feel okay laughing about because, thankfully, no one was seriously hurt. But it is also rather alarming. Are there really people who have taken Carrie Underwood's song "Jesus, Take the Wheel" and applied it literally to their lives? Does the Bible really teach Christians to "Let Go and Let God?"

And does that imply that real faith means sitting passively while God determines all the outcomes of our lives?

Cast Your Cares

As always, I want to begin by giving this cliché the benefit of the doubt. In most cases, when people use the phrase "let go and let God," it seems to me they are talking about worrying less and trusting God more. That is a very Biblical idea.

For instance, 1 Peter 5:7 says, "Cast all your anxiety on him because he cares for you."

Life is filled with many sources of stress. The Bible is aware of that. It frequently pictures the anxieties of this life as heavy burdens (Luke 21:34). These stresses can strangle faith (Matthew 13:22). We can all identify with the sleepless nights and aching stomachs that come from too much worry.

Peter's prescription is to remember that God cares for us. And, because God cares for us, we can transfer the burden of our anxieties and stresses to Him. By an act of faith, we can put our real anxieties on God and trust in His care.

There is a sense in which the Bible invites us to let God do our "worrying" for us. He carries the burden of our stress. We rest in His care. That's what we usually mean when we tell ourselves to "let go and let God."

Jesus says something very similar in the Sermon on the Mount. After talking about storing up treasures in heaven, He says, "Therefore I tell you, do not worry about your life, what you will eat or drink; or about your body, what you will wear. Is not life more important than food, and the body more important than clothes?" (Matthew 6:25).

Jesus wants us to know that the material world is not all that matters. There is more to life than stuff. Life is more important than food, and the body is more important than clothes. Real life—meaningful life—comes not from stuff, but from loving relationships, from selfless sacrifice, from a connection to God. Matter is not all that matters. The really meaningful stuff in life isn't stuff at all.

And so, we ought not to be anxious about food and clothing because food and clothing cannot provide the great things of life. Rather, we should transfer our worries about those things to our heavenly Father's gracious care, because He knows what we need.

"So do not worry, saying, 'What shall we eat?' or 'What shall we drink?' or 'What shall we wear?' For the pagans run after all these things, and your heavenly Father knows that you need them" (Matthew 6:31–32).

Our job is to seek God's priorities and will, trusting that the things we need will be provided as necessary. In other words, one might say that we need to "let go and let God."

"But seek first his kingdom and his righteousness, and all these things will be given to you as well" (Matthew 6:33).

The best reason to stop being anxious is that when we put our trust in Him, God makes sure we have what He wants us to have. It's a foolish thing to insist on carrying worrisome burdens which God has promised to carry for us when we put His kingly honor first in all that we do.

When used like this, the instruction to "let go and let God" aligns well with Biblical teaching.

If It's Not a Miracle, Does That Mean It Wasn't God?

And yet, the cliché is not a Bible verse and, taken to an extreme, it can be dangerous and absurd.

Clearly, a literal invitation to Jesus to take the wheel of a speeding car is foolishness. But there are many other examples of

Christians who have believed that trusting in God to act means they should take no action themselves.

Probably the most tragic is when children die of curable diseases because their parents refuse medical treatment out of a conviction that God will miraculously heal them. Every now and then one of these cases will receive national news coverage, as courts try to intervene in bringing life-saving medical attention before it is too late. Other times, the plight of the child doesn't reach public attention until death has already occurred.

For instance, a news station out of Philadelphia reports that two brothers died—four years apart—of treatable pneumonia and dehydration because their parents resorted to prayer instead of medical care.[4] Other stories of chemotherapy refused, burns left untreated, and corrective surgeries avoided have garnered national attention.[5]

It seems that believers can be so eager to show that God is capable of miraculous healing that they will, at times, forgo the established practices of modern medicine in the expectation of direct divine intervention. In some extreme communities, resorting to anything other than prayer and faith can be painted as rebellion against God.

This is the logic of "let go and let God" taken to very dark places.

Putting God to the Test

At Christmastime my first year of seminary, my maternal grandmother, Johanna Roghair, took ill and was hospitalized. Since I was on break from school, I was able to be home and I went with my mother to visit her. As we walked into the hospital room, my Mom said to her, "Russell is here. He's home from seminary. He can read scripture with you."

I remember feeling really awkward. Mom hadn't warned me that she was going to do that. I didn't feel that three months learning the Bible prepared me to pastor someone in their final moments on earth. And yet, here I was, and the person I was ministering to was my own grandmother.

I didn't know what to do. Grandma was pretty weak, and she wasn't talking much. But I asked her if she had a favorite Bible passage. She said Psalm 91.

At the time, Psalm 91 was not very familiar to me. But I looked it up, and I started reading it.

> Whoever dwells in the shelter of the Most High
>   will rest in the shadow of the Almighty.
> I will say of the Lord, "He is my refuge and my fortress,
>   my God, in whom I trust." (Psalm 91:1–2)

As I was reading, something remarkable happened. My grandmother, who was worn and tired, who would pass away less than 24 hours later, began reciting the Psalm with me. I was reading from the NIV while she was reciting the KJV, so the words didn't quite match up, but she prayed that Psalm with me. I was reading words on a page, she was singing songs from her heart.

And the thing about Psalm 91 is that it is filled with tremendous promises. Verse 3 says of God, "Surely he will save you from the fowler's snare and from the deadly pestilence."

A little later, verses 5 through 7 say,

> You will not fear the terror of night,
>   nor the arrow that flies by day,
> nor the pestilence that stalks in the darkness,
>   nor the plague that destroys at midday.
> A thousand may fall at your side,
>   ten thousand at your right hand,
>   but it will not come near you.

I have since heard Psalm 91 referred to as an "amulet" Psalm. Scholars believe that it was written during a time of national crisis, perhaps during the outbreak of a deadly disease as indicated by the words "pestilence" and "plague." The conjecture is that it was written as a prayer of protection, sort of like a magical amulet worn to ward off evil. People prayed it in the hope and belief that God would keep safe those who took their shelter in Him.

Like I said, the Psalm is filled with some tremendous promises:

- "no harm will overtake you" (v. 10)
- "no disaster will come near your tent" (v. 10)
- "you will not strike your foot against a stone" (v. 12)
- "you will tread on the lion and the cobra" (v. 13)

It sounds like the person who prays this Psalm with faith will never experience harm. It sounds like the perfect "let go and let God" Psalm. Make the Most High your dwelling and God will be with you in trouble. He will deliver and honor you (vss. 9, 15).

And yet, even as I read that Psalm to my grandmother, those of us in the room knew she was dying. She knew she was dying. There was no expectation that she would recover from her illness. But I didn't feel like God was breaking a promise to her, and neither did she. I believe God protected and saved her by ushering her into an eternity with Him.

It's interesting that the only time Psalm 91 gets quoted in the New Testament is in the story of Christ's temptations. In Matthew's telling, the second temptation involves the devil taking Jesus to the highest point of the temple in the holy city. There, from a spot where everyone can see Him, the devil invites Jesus to jump. And then he quotes Psalm 91:11–12. "He will command his angels concerning you, and they will lift you up in their hands, so that you will not strike your foot against a stone" (Matthew 4:6).

In other words, Satan is offering Jesus a shortcut to the throne. If He is really the Son of God, He can prove it by BASE jumping from the temple and letting the angels come and rescue Him. He can skip out on all the conflicts with the religious leaders and bypass the cross just by letting Psalm 91 come true in front of the entire city.

Jesus responds by quoting Deuteronomy 6:16. "Do not put the Lord your God to the test" (Matthew 4:7). Sure, Jesus could jump and wait for the angels to catch Him. They probably would.

But He's not about to test God in that way. He's not going to take some crazy chance just to prove His own faith in God or to make God prove Himself to Jesus.

Ordinary Means of Help

It seems to me that people who take the phrase "let go and let God" to its most radical applications—whether they are taking their hands off the steering wheel of a speeding car or resisting the use of modern medical science—are putting God to the test. They are demanding God intervene in extraordinary ways when He has already provided ordinary means of help.

There is a modern-day parable that I have heard often and repeated many times. You've probably heard a version of it as well.

> A man's house is in the path of a quickly rising flood. As he stands on his porch and watches the water fill his yard, some firefighters come by in a big SUV. They encourage the man to get into the truck so they can carry him to safety, but he refuses. "I've prayed to God," he says. "God will rescue me."
>
> Sometime later, the water has risen considerably and the man is now stationed at an upstairs window.

Some neighbors in a boat come by. They urge the man to get into the boat so they can carry him to safety, but he refuses. "I've prayed to God," he says. "God will rescue me."

Sometime later, the peak of the man's roof is all that is visible of the house. The man is clinging to his chimney when a helicopter comes by. A ladder is thrown down and the man is urged to grab on so that the helicopter can carry him to safety. But he refuses. "I've prayed to God," he says. "God will rescue me."

Sometime later, after the man has drowned, he arrives at the heavenly gates. There, he is met by God. The man says, "God, I believed with all my heart that you would rescue me. I put my full faith in you. Why didn't you save me from the flood?" And God's answer is, "I sent a truck, I sent a boat, I sent a helicopter. What more did you want Me to do?"

That's the story I think of when I hear about people refusing to seek medical treatment or declining to take basic precautions against illness or accidents. I want to ask those people, "Why are you putting God to the test? Why are you requiring God to intervene in some miraculous way when already proven means of protection are right there in front of you?"

Trust Like the Birds

Is there a better perspective offered in the Bible? What can we say about the relationship between trusting God fully and personal responsibility?

If we return to what Jesus says in the Sermon on the Mount, we can see an interesting lesson in the way Jesus chooses to illustrate his teaching on not worrying. He says, "Look at the birds of the air; they do not sow or reap or store away in barns, and yet your heavenly Father feeds them. Are you not much more valuable than they?" (Matthew 6:26).

Larry Burkett, the late financial planner who founded Crown Financial Ministries, wrote about some of the clients who came to him with what he called the "birds-in-the-field" syndrome. These clients came to him with no savings, no plan for their retirement, and a lot more debt than they could afford. And when he'd question them about it, they'd point to Matthew chapter 6 and say that God takes care of the birds and flowers, certainly He'd take care of them.

But, Burkett would point out, you rarely see a lazy bird. While God provides the worms and the seeds, still the birds are out there gathering and working. There's a reason we say "the early bird gets the worm," because birds tend to be up long before you or me, gathering their meals.

There's a difference between faith and presumption. Faith trusts that as we seek God's will and follow His leadings He will provide us with what we need. Presumption, on the other hand, makes all sorts of terrible decisions and then expects God to make up for all our losses.

For example:

- If you lose your job and start delivering pizzas and stocking shelves during the midnight shift and trust God to provide—that's faith.
- On the other hand, if you lose your job and spend your day sitting on the couch playing video games and eating Doritos and expect God to provide—that's presumption.
- If you go from giving whatever happens to be in your wallet when the offering plate passes by to giving 10% at the

beginning of every month and trusting that God will provide—that's faith.

- But if you charge a $1500 flat-screen to your credit card when you don't have the money and expect God to provide—that's presumption.
- If you give up your job and move to a smaller house so you can start attending seminary and you trust God to provide—that's faith.
- But if you buy a huge house with no money down and huge balloon payments at the end and expect God to provide— that's presumption.

Faith is not an excuse for laziness. Neither is it a guarantee that God will bless our bad decisions. Burkett wrote, "Too often Christians borrow to do what they themselves desire, and expect God to rescue them when the bills arrive. To 'believe' requires faith; to charge is presumption."[6]

Or again, if we return to 1 Peter 5:7 and look at it in context, we see that casting our cares on God is not an excuse for passivity.

"Cast all your anxiety on him because he cares for you. Be alert and of sober mind. Your enemy the devil prowls around like a roaring lion looking for someone to devour. Resist him, standing firm in the faith..." (1 Peter 5:7–9).

Notice the active verbs in verses 8 and 9: "Be alert." "[Be] of sober mind." "Resist." "Stand firm." In the web series "Look at the Book," Pastor John Piper states,

> When God says "I will protect you. Don't worry. Don't have anxieties. I will protect you" The result is not "no warfare." The result is "fight!" And "fight to win!" You don't fight out of anxiety, you fight out of watchfulness. When you are watchful you don't have

to be anxious. When you are sober minded you don't have to be anxious. But you do have to fight!

...all your anxieties have gone onto God. He's now caring for you. He's fighting for you. He's strong for you. But that doesn't make you careless, it doesn't make you passive. It makes you fight! Mighty to resist the devil![7]

Confidence that God is in control should not make Christians passive, rather it should spur us on to be that much more active in caring for ourselves and doing God's will.

Trust God and Get Going

It occurs to me that the first two clichés we have looked at are essentially polar opposites of each other. Together, they represent one of the tensions that has run through Christianity ever since Jesus ascended back to heaven.

Is the Christian life best described by "God helps those who help themselves" or "Let go and let God?" That is, is salvation by grace or by works? Is the Christian life about restful trust or striving obedience? Do we express our commitment to God by doing all that we can for Him and for ourselves? Or do we best show our loyalty when we lay back so that His power is shown in our weakness?

Every generation of the Church has wrestled with these questions. Sometimes we are tempted to emphasize the need for our effort and responsibility. Other times we want to highlight God's sovereignty and grace.

And yet, it seems that the Bible has no problem putting these two apparently opposite ideas together. What we see as contradictory the Bible treats as complementary. God's rule in our life and world does not eliminate the need for human effort, it inspires it. Salvation by grace does not cancel good works, it prepares the way for them (see Ephesians 2:8–10). It's because God provides for the birds that they go out to gather their food. It's because God cares for us that we can stand firm against the devil.

Philippians 2:12–13 places these two ideas side by side without tension.

> Therefore, my dear friends, as you have always obeyed—not only in my presence, but now much more in my absence—continue to work out your salvation with fear and trembling, [13] for it is God who works in you to will and to act in order to fulfill his good purpose.

The key word is the word that starts verse 13, "for." That gives us our motivation, our reason. We are called to work out our salvation—our obedience—not to earn it, but because we already have it. "My dear friends...work...*for* it is God who works in you."

It's not just, "Get to work, because God helps those who help themselves." Neither is it, "Sit back and watch God, because the less we do the more He shines through." Rather, as J.I. Packer notably said, "The Christian's motto should not be 'Let go and let God' but 'Trust God and get going.'"[8]

For further study, see the Discussion Guide for Chapter 2 on page 129.

– 3 –

GOD JUST WANTS ME TO BE HAPPY

The Pursuit of Happiness

I'll never forget the conversation. It was late in the afternoon of a crisp fall day. I was standing on my front steps talking to a deacon who lived just down the road from me. He had come to tell me he was quitting leadership and leaving the church.

The reason? He was moving out of the home he shared with his wife and his two teenage children and moving in with another woman.

He knew his decision was not acceptable behavior for a believer, much less a deacon. He knew the Bible said it was wrong. He knew he was burning bridges with friends and siblings and even his own parents. Nothing I said to him was new information.

I asked, "Why?" If he knew all these things to be true, why was he doing it?

"Because," he said, "I'm not happy with my wife. But my girlfriend makes me happy. And I believe God just wants me to be happy."

*****

Was he right? Is our happiness God's greatest desire for us? Do all other considerations take a back seat to our desire for fun?

I believe the idea that God just wants us to be happy is a Christian myth. It comes through in a number of clichés, secular and Christian. "If it feels right, do it." "If God didn't want you to do it, He would not have made it so much fun!" "Whatever makes you happy."

The logic works like this: Happiness is good. God is also good. Therefore, God must want me to be happy.

More than that, here in America, we feel like happiness is a birthright. The Declaration of Independence says that we are all endowed with the unalienable right to life, liberty, and the pursuit of happiness.

Many of the things marketed to us are sold with the implicit promise that they will make us happy.

- Feeling a little blah? Spend a weekend in Vegas. And remember, what happens there stays there.
- The routines of life got you stuck in a rut? Give this sports car a try and feel the exhilaration of endless horsepower and a finely appointed interior.
- Tired of everybody telling you what to do? Head to your favorite fast food joint and have it your way!

Happiness is so vital to our way of life that it feels almost unpatriotic not to be seeking things that make us happy all of the time. We believe so strongly in the endless pursuit of happiness that we've stamped all things happy with God's seal of approval.

#Blessed

This cliché is tricky, because I don't want to give the impression that God wants us to be unhappy.

I realize a lot of people have been raised with that impression of God. Some people have had such bad experiences with strict churches or overzealous parents that they can only imagine God as a kind of supreme killjoy, who sits in heaven and watches for the slightest sign of fun, then reaches down and swats us—like He's got one of those portable bug zappers.

It is vital for us to know that God is NOT opposed to our happiness. He is not offended when we smile or laugh or do something that brings us pleasure.

In fact, the Bible is unblushing in its use of words like "pleasure" (see Psalm 16:11); "delight" (see Psalm 37:2); "satisfaction" (see Psalm 17:15); and "gladness" (see Psalm 45:15). It was God who created the first man and woman and sexual union and pronounced it all "very good" (see Genesis 1:31 and 2:24). The calendar of ancient Israel was filled with mandatory periods of rest and celebration at God's command (see Leviticus 23). Jesus' first public miracle took place at a party and involved keeping the wine flowing (see John 2:1–11).

God is not the cosmic hall monitor. He is not waiting in heaven to hand out demerits anytime He sees us having fun.

The Hebrew word often translated "blessed" in the Old Testament is a word that could also be translated as "happy." I remember taking a class on the Psalms with Dr. Ray Ortlund, Jr. where he was practically coming out of his shoes with excitement as he covered Psalm 1:1–2:

> Blessed is the one
>> who does not walk in step with the wicked

or stand in the way that sinners take
 or sit in the company of mockers,
but whose delight is in the law of the Lord,
 and who meditates on his law day and night.

"Blessed means happy!" Dr. Ortlund told us. "This describes a person who is living a life worthy of congratulations! A person who is to be envied! A person who is living the best life possible!"

The metaphor the psalmist uses in verse 3 is a tree planted by streams of water. The picture is of a life that is fruitful and drought-resistant. A happy life. Supremely blessed, fortunate, well-off, and flourishing. That's what God wants for us.

This blessed state is not a matter of "whatever makes you happy" though. Notice that the person described in the Psalm is one "whose delight is in the law of the Lord." The Bible recognizes that true happiness is found when we live in a way consistent with God's designs for us and the world.

In an essay written for Ligonier ministries, Ken Myers says:

> When Thomas Jefferson selected the phrase "the pursuit of happiness" to describe one of the unalienable rights of man, he was appropriating an idea with a very long history. Since the time of Aristotle and before, happiness was understood as a condition to which all people properly aspire. But for the Greeks, as for the biblical writers, happiness was an objective reality, not just a feeling or an emotional state.

In other words, he says, happiness is an "ethical, not a psychological project." The modern sense of happiness as feeling good all the time has overtaken the ancient notion of finding satisfaction in believing and doing the right things.[9]

Happy Mistakes

What happens when we make the emotional state of "happy" the highest goal in life?

I can think of at least three problems that come when we start believing that God just wants us to be happy.

1. We Fake Happiness

If you are Christian, and you believe that God really wants you to be happy, then you might feel pressure to pretend to be happy, even when you're not.

Tell me if this sounds familiar. You slept a little late on a Sunday morning. The kids did not want to eat what was offered for breakfast and did not want to wear the clothes you set out for them. On the ride to church you got into a fight with your spouse. By the time the car pulls into the parking lot, the littlest is crying, the other two are screaming at each other, and you and your spouse are not talking. Then you turn and say to everybody, "We're going to church now, so get happy!"

Because we believe God wants us happy, we put on a false front of happiness whenever we are at church or around church friends. People greet us in the halls and say, "How's it going?" and the answer is always, "Great, just great!" even when we are not, actually, doing all that great.

Sometimes, when we're around people that we know don't believe in Jesus—and we're trying to invite them to church or show Jesus to them—we feel like we have to be happy all the time. We figure the best advertisement for Jesus will be to show them how happy we are. God wants us to be happy, we figure, so we better show people that it's working.

But here's the thing: it's not real. And people can tell when we're faking it. They aren't looking for insincere, plastered-on smiles. They're looking for genuine, real people who have genuine, real problems.

Ruth Graham, daughter of Billy Graham, did a series of speaking engagements after her first marriage ended with her husband's affair and her second ended when her husband became abusive. At first she felt she needed to hide. Her history hardly fit the image of America's most prominent Christian family. Then she decided she had a story to share. As she explained to the *Christian Post*:

> "The world is tired of plastic Christians. I was tired of being a plastic Christian. I told everybody I had it all together, and I was falling apart. And I was scared to death to tell somebody.
>
> "I think I'm dealing with believers already who are just struggling in their lives like I did.... A lot of people have been taught that if you're depressed there's something wrong with you spiritually. That's so unfair. It's a physical issue....
>
> "[You] live up to people's expectations, and you become inauthentic and you pretend you have it all together, but inside you're dying."[10]

If we buy into the myth that says God just wants us to be happy, we might be tempted to fake being happy even when we are not. We lie to ourselves, we lie to others, and we give a hollowed-out impression of what Christianity really is.

2. We Chase Happiness

A second problem with this myth is that it may lead us in an unfulfilling quest for happiness. If we believe that the most important thing in life is to feel happy, we'll try experience after experience in order to find happiness.

That's what happened to the Teacher in the book of Ecclesiastes. Ecclesiastes is all about the apparent absurdity of life. In chapter 2, the Teacher goes on a quest for pleasure. He tries laughter. He indulges himself with wine. He undertakes great projects—houses and vineyards, gardens and parks and fruit trees. He buys slaves. He owns flocks and herds. He amasses gold and silver, the treasure of kings and provinces. He brings in the best singers. He brings in hundreds of women to form his own harem. He becomes, in his words, "greater by far than anyone in Jerusalem" before him (Ecclesiastes 2:9).

And yet, this is his conclusion in the next verses:

> I denied myself nothing my eyes desired;
>   I refused my heart no pleasure.
> My heart took delight in all my labor,
>   and this was the reward for all my toil.
> Yet when I surveyed all that my hands had done
>   and what I had toiled to achieve,
> everything was meaningless, a chasing after the wind;
>   nothing was gained under the sun.
> (Ecclesiastes 2:10–11)

After trying everything he could get his hands on, he found he had not gained anything. The Teacher in Ecclesiastes discovered the truth that everybody who has ever chased happiness has discovered—it is temporary, it doesn't last, and it only leaves you wanting more. Chasing happiness is like chasing the wind.

The Harvard Study of Adult Development is the longest continuous study of adulthood ever attempted. Beginning in 1938, researchers began tracking 268 Harvard sophomores—some of the brightest and wealthiest young men in the world—as well as 456 boys from inner city Boston—some of the poorest and most disadvantaged people in America. Every two years for the rest of their lives these men were asked to complete a survey. Researchers also studied their medical records, regularly conducted in-person interviews, talked with their wives and other close family members, and in later years studied x-rays, echocardiograms, and brain scans. Today, less than 10% of the original subjects are still alive, but researchers are continuing the study with their children and grandchildren.

In an interview with Dr. Laurie Santos on "The Happiness Lab" podcast, the director of the study, Dr. Robert Waldinger, says many of their findings are not surprising. Smoking was bad for the health of the participants. As was alcoholism.

But other things were surprising. In a study of some of the most privileged and some of the most vulnerable men in America over the course of eight decades, the study found very little correlation between how much stuff a person had and how happy they reported being. Dr. Waldinger says, "Wealth does not make people happy. Having your material needs met does make you happy. Once you get there, making more money does not make you appreciably more happy."

In many ways, Dr. Waldinger sounds like the Teacher of Ecclesiastes. He says, "Winning the Nobel Prize doesn't make you happier. Winning the lottery doesn't make you happier. It's not the things we imagine, it's not the shiny baubles that make us happy."

Instead, Dr. Waldinger says that the strongest sense of well-being and satisfaction in life came from those who had the strongest and most enduring relationships.

> "Our men, as they were looking back on their lives, as they were at the end of their lives, said the things they were proudest of were building a family, raising healthy children, having a strong relationship with a

partner, teaching their grandchildren to sail. These were the things they talked about. They didn't talk about how much they achieved at work or how much money they made."

When we chase happiness in material things or bigger and better experiences, we end up, as the podcast host says, "putting a lot of time and effort into improving our happiness using strategies that will not succeed."[11]

3. We Bow to Happiness

Probably the biggest danger with this myth is that it can lead us to justify all sorts of questionable decisions on the basis of doing what makes us happy.

This is what the deacon on my front steps was doing. He believed the myth and bought the t-shirt. He couldn't believe God would want him to give up something that made him feel so good. If it was really wrong, he figured God would make him unhappy. But as it was, this is what felt right, and he was going for it.

In the book of Philippians, Paul writes about those who live as enemies of the cross of Jesus. He says about them: "Their destiny is destruction, their god is their stomach, and their glory is in their shame. Their mind is set on earthly things" (Philippians 3:19).

When we believe that the most important thing God wants for us in life is our happiness, we have a tendency to make gods out of our appetites. We direct our lives by what feels best.

What Could be Better than Happiness?

Those are some of the problems with living by this cliché. But if God's greatest desire for us is not happiness, what does He want for us? What could be better than happiness?

43

I think if we really searched the Bible, we could generate quite a list of things that are more important to God than our happiness. But I've thought of three things that correspond to the three problems we just covered.

1. Honesty

I think God wants us to be honest with ourselves, with others, and with Him about how we are feeling. I don't think God wants "happy plastic people" wearing pretend smiles and forcing a silver lining onto everything that happens.

I say that because of the honesty of the Bible. Of the 150 poems that make up the book of Psalms, at least one-third of them can be classified as laments. That is, they are poems that start out not by praising God, not by telling God how great He is, but by complaining about how rotten things are.

Take Psalm 55 for example. Here's how it starts (vss. 1–2):

> Listen to my prayer, O God,
>   do not ignore my plea;
> hear me and answer me.
> My thoughts trouble me and I am distraught.

The Psalms can be almost startling in their honesty. David isn't having a good day and is not afraid to tell God about it. He goes on:

> My heart is in anguish within me;
>   the terrors of death have fallen on me.
> Fear and trembling have beset me;
>   horror has overwhelmed me. (Psalm 55:4–5)

I'm guessing if you'd asked David how things were going on the day he wrote this, he wouldn't have smiled and said, "Great, just great."

Now, I realize that when you ask someone how they are doing, you don't really want to hear a litany of their latest troubles. There's some social convention there.

But there also needs to be a place in Christianity for honest lament and reflection on the genuine hurts in life. The church should be a community where we can bring our brokenness and pain. We don't have to force happiness when it's not there. God doesn't want us to be faking it.

2. Trust

Instead of chasing after the next great experience all the time, or trying to capture that elusive happiness, God asks us to trust that He will provide us with what we need.

Hebrews 11 shares with us a great illustration taken from the life of Moses:

> By faith Moses, when he had grown up, refused to be known as the son of Pharaoh's daughter. He chose to be mistreated along with the people of God rather than to enjoy the fleeting pleasures of sin. He regarded disgrace for the sake of Christ as of greater value than the treasures of Egypt, because he was looking ahead to his reward. (Hebrews 11:24–26)

As a Prince of Egypt, Moses had the opportunity to chase happiness wherever he thought he might find it. But rather than enjoy the pleasures of sin for a short time, he trusted that God had a reward that would be worth waiting for. So he traded in the palace for wandering in the desert.

In the same way, God wants us to trust that He knows what is best for us. He wants us to view long-term joy as of more value than short-term pleasures.

3. Obedience

Often when I hear somebody say, "I believe God just wants me to be happy" I know they are trying to justify something both they and I know is wrong. It really means that they don't care what God wants at that moment, they are only concerned with what they want.

But when those situations arise, the Bible is pretty clear about what God wants from us. Jesus says:

> "If you love me, keep my commands...Anyone who loves me will obey my teaching. My Father will love them, and we will come to them and make our home with them. Anyone who does not love me will not obey my teaching. These words you hear are not my own; they belong to the Father who sent me." (John 14:15, 23–24)

Clearly, our faith expressed through obedience is more important to God than our short-term happiness.

Now, don't get me wrong. I'm not saying that obedience will always be unpleasant. Often, doing the right thing is also the thing that will make us the most happy—if not immediately, then almost certainly in the long-run.

But if it comes down to a choice between doing what God says is right, and doing something that we think will make us happy right now, God asks us to choose obedience. Even if we don't feel great about it at the moment. Even if we're not sure how it will work out.

Happiness vs. Joy

The idea that what God most wants for us in life is our happiness is a myth. It can lead us to fake happiness, to chase it, or bow down to it. We can end up shaping our lives in ways that have little to do with what God actually says.

But, again, I don't want you to think that God is opposed to anything good in life. I don't want you to get the impression that Christianity is a giant, fun-free zone. I don't want you to think that God is all dour and grim and severe.

Because that's not true. In fact, I think there is one more thing God wants for us far more than happiness … and that's joy.

It's important for us to see that there is a difference between happiness and joy. Whenever you are happy, you are probably also experiencing joy. But joy is something you can also experience even when you are not happy. Happiness, as the modern world tends to define it, is temporary. You see it in the word itself: Happiness = what's "happening." If you say, "I'm happy" you're really saying, "I feel good, right now." Happiness is dependent on circumstances.

But joy is different. It's deeper. It lasts even in the midst of the trials of life. Joy isn't dependent on circumstances. Joy is strength. Joy is internal. Joy is eternal.

- It's possible to have joy even when we are being honest about difficulties we are facing.
- It's possible to have joy even as we are trusting God for something better.
- It's possible to have joy even as we refuse to enjoy something we know is wrong in order to obey what is right.

Joy doesn't come from what is happening now, but instead comes from the firm conviction that Jesus has all that we need.

Here's what Jesus said:

> If you keep my commands, you will remain in my love, just as I have kept my Father's commands and

remain in his love. I have told you this so that my joy may be in you and that your joy may be complete. (John 15:10–11)

Jesus came, not so that we could be happy—though He's not opposed to us being happy—but so that we could have joy. And that's much better.

For further study, see the Discussion Guide for Chapter 3 on page 132.

– 4 –
TIME HEALS ALL WOUNDS

Iron Mike

Mike Ditka is a man's man. A Hall of Fame football player, he was the 1961 Rookie of the Year and won a championship with the Chicago Bears in 1963. Five times he made the Pro Bowl and five times he was chosen as the NFL's First Team All-Pro tight end. When his playing days were over he moved into coaching, eventually becoming the hard-nosed head coach of the team he starred for as a player.

He coached the Bears for 11 years, living up to his nickname of "Iron Mike" with a blunt style of speaking to the press and a fiery demeanor on the sideline. He won the championship in 1985 with the "Super Bowl shuffling" team of Walter Payton, Jim McMahon, Mike Singletary, and William "the Refrigerator" Perry.

With a blue-collar personality, Ditka was beloved in Chicago. He inspired a recurring *Saturday Night Live* sketch in which portly men with broom brush mustaches would sit around a Chicago sports bar and extol the virtues of "da Bears!"

Like I said, he was a man's man. And, for many, he symbolized old school football, where the game was a miniature version of war, with men playing through injuries and engaging in personal combat play after play. Mike Ditka was tough.

But on January 5, 1993, after the Bears had finished a disappointing 5 and 11 season, Mike Ditka was fired. And as he stepped to the podium at the press conference where his termination was announced, Iron Mike Ditka was visibly upset. With tears in his eyes and a shaking voice, he said, "I'll try to do this with class. Scripture tells you that all things shall pass. This, too, shall pass."[12]

Suddenly, sportswriters from all over Chicago were scrambling for their Bibles, searching their concordances so they could accurately quote the Bible verse Ditka was citing.

But the thing was, nobody could find it. Because the phrase, "This, too, shall pass," is not in the Bible.

Looking for Something to Say

Let's go back to the scenario described in the Introduction. Let's say you are talking to someone who has just experienced grief. Maybe it is someone, like Coach Ditka, who has unexpectedly lost a job. Maybe it is someone who has just had a relationship end—a break-up, or a divorce. Or maybe it is someone who has just experienced the passing of a loved one—a parent has died, or a spouse, or a child.

Whatever the case, this person you are talking with is obviously distraught. The grief is heavy, the sadness is evident. And you want to be of some comfort. You want to say something that will lighten the load and ease the sorrow.

But you don't know quite what to say. All your words seem clumsy. Nothing seems good enough. Your friend keeps saying things like, "I don't know if I will ever get over this" or "I don't see how I can go on."

You want to be helpful so, finally, you lean in and you give a half-hug and you say something like, "Just give it time." Or, "Things will get easier." Or, even like Coach Ditka, you say, "There, there. This too shall pass."

This chapter is about a whole range of time-related clichés that we tend to use in the face of grief. I'll capture the essence of the notion with the phrase, "Time heals all wounds."

Scabs and Scars

When I was five or six years old my family went on a camping trip with my cousins' family. One day, while I was riding my bicycle on the steep gravel road that led from the campground down to the beach, I wiped out.

My little body went sprawling and I slid several yards on the loose rock. Because I was wearing only swim trunks at the time, my right side was covered with a nasty case of road rash from my hip bone to my armpit.

At the time, I thought it was the worst accident ever. I thought I would be disfigured for life. I was certain I needed to be brought to the hospital for round after round of treatment. Instead, my mom and my aunt picked the bits of sand and stone out of the wound, gently washed it with a damp towel, placed large band-aids over the worst scrapes, gave me a children's Tylenol, and forgot all about it.

As it turned out, by the time we got home from our camping weekend, the scrapes had scabbed over. Within a week of getting home, only one or two of the deepest gashes were still visible. By the end of the month, all that remained of the accident were a few white patches where my new skin was less tan than the rest of me. Today, 40 plus years later, I don't have any scars from that childhood biking accident at all.

It seemed like it was time that healed my wound. Technically speaking, that's not true. Rather, it was the incredible healing mechanisms God built into my anatomy. Platelets gathered at the injury site to form scabs, my immune system protected against infection, and red blood cells set about the work of rebuilding my injured skin.

In healthy bodies this process happens naturally and without conscious direction on our part. It appears to be a function of the passage of time. Given enough time, most physical wounds heal on their own.

In the same way, we assume the passage of time also brings healing for emotional and relational pain. When the wound is fresh, it hurts a lot. But give it time, and we'll get over it.

It's a nice enough thought. And, in its own way, I suppose it gives a measure of hope. But again, just to be clear, "Time heals all wounds" is not in the Bible. Neither is, "This, too, shall pass." And ultimately, I think phrases like this do more harm than good.

Our Times Are in His Hands

Before we begin looking at the problems with these time-related clichés, let's ask, is there any Biblical truth? Is there anything about this notion that matches up with Biblical teaching?

And the answer is, not really. The idea of time healing wounds is just not in the Bible.

As with, "God helps those who help themselves," the origin of this proverb is thought to trace back to Ancient Greece. A playwright named Menander, who lived about 300 years before Jesus, is credited with writing the line, "Time is the healer of all necessary evils."

In English, Geoffrey Chaucer, from the 1300s, wrote that: "as time him hurt, / a time does him cure."

From there, "time heals all wounds" just seems to have become an accepted proverb.

But if we look at what the Bible says about time, we really cannot find this idea. The Bible's view of time is that it is under the control of God. A representative verse is Psalm 31:15: "My times are in your hands; deliver me from the hands of my enemies, from those who pursue me."

The idea is that God determines the number of days we have to live, that He knows the plans He has for us during that time, and that He wants us to make the most of the time we have. Psalm 90:12 expresses the attitude that we should have toward time: "Teach us to number our days, that we may gain a heart of wisdom."

The better we understand that God controls our time on earth, the better use we will be able to make of the time we have.

That's what the Bible says about time. But on the question of what the passage of time does for our pain, the Bible says nothing.

The other statement, the one that Mike Ditka attributed to the Bible, actually comes from a Persian legend from about 800 years ago. The story goes that a king called all his advisors and wise men to him and asked them for one true statement that could be applied to every situation. The wise men consulted with each other and threw themselves into deep contemplation before finally returning to the king with this phrase, "This, too, shall pass." Supposedly, the king was so impressed that he had it inscribed on a ring.

It's an old idea, with New Age vibes. The point it makes is, no matter what situation we find ourselves in, we should remember that it will eventually come to an end. If we are having a great time, if we are experiencing the greatest joy we have ever experienced, we should not get too carried away, because it will pass. And likewise, if we are having a terrible time, if we are caught up in grief, we should not get too sad, because it will also pass.

As another non-Biblical saying has it, nothing lasts forever.

Ditka probably confused the saying with a Bible verse because the language sounds like something in the King James Bible. The KJV often uses the phrase, "And it came to pass."

But "This, too, shall pass" is not in the Bible, and the idea it expresses of not getting too high or low isn't really in the Bible either. The closest we get is 2 Corinthian 4:17–18:

> For our light and momentary troubles are achieving for us an eternal glory that far outweighs them all. So we fix our eyes not on what is seen, but on what is unseen, since what is seen is temporary, but what is unseen is eternal.

This verse conveys the idea that the things of this life only last for a while. But instead of the notion that we shouldn't get too attached, the Bible comes from the perspective that says the experiences of this life are preparation for an eternal glory in the next life. It's not about waiting things out down here so much as it is keeping our eyes fixed on our coming hope.

Our first question, then, is: Is there any Biblical truth in the phrase "Time heals all wounds?" Our answer needs to be, "Very little." This is really not a Biblical idea.

Waiting for a Flat Tire to Reinflate

Which leads to our second question: What is wrong with this phrase? Where does it get off track?

As I studied it, the thing that stood out to me is that nobody likes this phrase. As common as the saying is, as often as we hear it, there is no one on the internet—Christian or non-Christian—defending it as helpful.

For one thing, it is empirically false. If the saying "Time heals all wounds" were true, then adults would be demonstrably more joyful than children. That is to say, adults have had more time to experience hurt, but they have also had more time to be healed from that hurt. Children, on the other hand, have barely had any time to recover from whatever wounds they have experienced, and so we should expect them to be more heavily weighed down. Since that is not our usual observation—in general, children are more joyful than adults—it should call into question the idea that time is the key factor in our healing.

Moreover, the phrase is just not that helpful. If you have ever experienced significant grief and someone has told you, "It will get better with time" or "Just give it time" you know that raises all kinds of questions. How much time? And if a significant amount of time has passed and you still feel the pain, does that mean something is wrong with you?

The notion that "Time heals all wounds" really implies that when we are in grief we will be allowed a certain amount of time to be sad, but after that (and nobody says just how long) the implication is that we should "get over it" or "snap out of it."

Rose Kennedy, the mother of two sons who were assassinated (John F. Kennedy and Robert F. Kennedy), is quoted quite often on this subject. She said: "It has been said 'time heals all wounds.' I do not agree. The wounds remain. In time, the mind, protecting its sanity, covers them with scar tissue and the pain lessens. But it never goes away."[13]

The passage of time can distance us from our hurts, it may soften the pain we feel, but time is never enough to heal our wounds.

Secular psychologists remind us that grieving is an active process. In any other part of our life, we do not simply sit around and expect the passage of time to make everything better. An article in "Psychology Today" gives these examples:

We have to *look* for a new job, *search* for the right house, *study* to get through school. Even if we want to win the lottery, we still have to *buy* the ticket. We have to take the initiative to do something to cause something else to happen. Is grief different? Can it really be true that time alone is enough for grief to go away? I don't think so....[14]

Another article I found gave the example of a flat tire. If you go to your driveway and find a flat tire on your car, will you just stand there and wait for it to reinflate? If you do, you'll be standing there for a while. Instead, you will do something. You will call a mechanic, get an air tank, put on the spare. You'll take some initiative.[15]

The "Psychology Today" article goes on:

> The point here, though, is that time does NOT heal all wounds. A more apt saying is "IT'S WHAT YOU DO WITH THE TIME THAT HEALS." Like any other aspect of life, mourning is an active, working process, not a passive one.[16]

I think that is both true and helpful. From a non-Christian perspective, the best way to find healing in grief is to engage the grieving process. And that applies to Christians as well. Don't just wait for the passing of time, work through your feelings.

But is that it? Is that all the hope we can give?

The Wounded Healer

This leads directly to our third question: Is there better news in the gospel? If we reject the idea that time is the healer of all wounds, does the Bible offer something better?

The answer, of course, is "YES!" The Bible does not tell us to look to our clocks or calendars for healing, but to look to God. Psalm 147:3 says: "He heals the brokenhearted and binds up their wounds."

One of the most important things we can do to work through our grief is bring it to God. It is His grace and love that can remove some of the heartache we feel. Yes, time can be a factor in receiving the comfort of God, but through God's grace we can find the ability to rejoice in both the good times and the bad.

Quite frankly, I don't even know if "healing wounds" is the correct language to be using. I lost my father more than a decade ago, at an age that I consider to be too young. And I don't know if I want to say that I am over it, or that the wound has completely healed, because to say such things would feel like I am saying that I don't miss him, or that he has somehow ceased to matter to me. Those things are not true. I feel like I will carry the pain of losing my father for the rest of my life. But, at the same time, I know that God is walking through that pain with me.

Let me share with you another relevant scripture, this one from Isaiah 61. This is a passage that Jesus quoted at the beginning of His public ministry. In some ways, this passage is what Jesus identified as His purpose statement, His reason for coming into the world:

> The Spirit of the Sovereign Lord is on me,
>   because the Lord has anointed me
>   to proclaim good news to the poor.
> He has sent me to bind up the brokenhearted,
>   to proclaim freedom for the captives
>   and release from darkness for the prisoners,
> to proclaim the year of the Lord's favor
>   and the day of vengeance of our God,
> to comfort all who mourn.... (Isaiah 61:1–2)

Notice those lines, "to bind up the brokenhearted" and "to comfort all who mourn." Jesus came into the world to walk with us in our times of grief. He came to support us in our pain. For me, I'm not looking to "get over" my Dad's death, but I take great comfort in the fact that Jesus is there to support me.

Billy Graham said this about mourning: "If there is something we need more than anything else during grief, it's a friend who stands with us, who doesn't leave us. Jesus is that friend."[17]

Another scripture, 1 Peter 2:24, says: "'He himself bore our sins' in his body on the cross, so that we might die to sins and live for righteousness; 'by his wounds you have been healed.'"

The good news of the gospel is that Jesus came to identify with us in our pain and grief. The quotes in this verse are from Isaiah 53, which also tells us that Jesus was "a man of sorrows" and "familiar with suffering" (Isaiah 53:3). The reminder, here, is that Jesus heals our wounds through His own woundedness. He is not an impassive observer of our pain, but He has experienced pain Himself.

Australian radio broadcaster Chris Witts says:

> When we tell people time heals all wounds we discount a Wounded Healer, who came to restore the deepest parts of our stories. We look to time to save us instead of a God who so graciously already did. He sent Jesus Christ into our world. He suffered and died for our sins. He knows about being wounded. We look at our clocks and ask them to wipe our tears away when we have a Savior who promises He will. Time can't heal me. Time can't make me better. But there is Someone who can. I can't keep putting my hope in time. It will continue to fail me and continue to rip open the tender places in my heart. But I do

believe in a God who was wounded so He could heal
me. That is something that won't disappoint.[18]

Your wounds may be a couple of days old, or a couple of months, or
a couple of years, or even a couple of decades. However much time
has passed, it's possible that those wounds still have the potential
to hurt as much as the day you first received them. Time is not the
determining factor here.

But the good news of the Bible is that Jesus knows about your
pain. He wants to walk with you through it. He knows what it is like
to be wounded. He is the friend who stands with you. He is the
friend who won't leave you.

Here's the main point of this chapter. Here's the one thing I
hope you will hold on to from this study:

> *Time does not heal all wounds,*
> *but Jesus, the Wounded Healer, does.*

Take your pain to Jesus. Just like you wouldn't stand around
waiting for your tire to reinflate, don't sit around waiting for time
to numb your grief. Instead, take it to the one who was wounded
for your healing. Take it to the one who came to bind up your
broken heart.

You might always have your pain with you, but Jesus wants to
walk with you and help you carry that pain.

What to Say

Finally, I want to go back to the scenario that I described at the
beginning of the chapter, where you are attempting to comfort
someone who is dealing with grief. If you've been in that situation,
you know it is sometimes difficult to find the right words to say. It's

often in that awkwardness that we say something unhelpful like, "Time heals all wounds."

If we don't want to "sing songs to a heavy heart," what do we do? How can we be a source of comfort in the midst of sorrow?

As I was researching this cliché I came across an article written by Victoria Strong. When Victoria's daughter, Gwendolyn, was eight weeks old she suddenly began struggling to breathe. It turned out that she had Spinal Muscular Atrophy (SMA), a genetic condition that meant she was essentially paralyzed. Gwendolyn lived until the age of seven, never able to walk, never able to talk, never any hope of a long-term cure. Her parents set up a foundation, and they continue to advocate for SMA research and support.

The blog post addressed the myth that time heals all wounds. And in it—speaking as a mother who has endured the greatest of tragedies—Victoria Strong suggests some ways that we can come alongside those who are grieving.[19] I thought it was helpful, so here are three things she suggests:

1) Say names.

Sometimes, we are reluctant to bring up someone who has passed away because we are afraid we will reopen old wounds. We think that by not mentioning the names of those who have died we are sparing our friends the pain of thinking about them. Victoria Strong writes:

> Whether it has been one month, five years, ten years—speak of them. You aren't bringing up a sensitive topic or bad memories. There will never ever be a day our child is not on our mind. Parents may cry hearing their child's name spoken aloud, but these types of tears are fresh glue to a broken heart that will never be fully mended.[20]

Personally, I welcome it when people want to talk about my Dad. When I hear memories that others have of him, or find out that somebody else misses him too, that brings me comfort. Even when I am talking with someone who never knew him, it is nice when they acknowledge that I must miss him.

2) Remember dates.

On holidays, anniversaries, birthdays, the date of death. When you know that these days are going to be hard, when you know that a person is going to be especially missed, say something. Again, there is enormous comfort in knowing that someone else is aware of our pain. It is so meaningful to know someone else is thinking of us as we are thinking of those who are gone.

You are not reopening old wounds. Those wounds are going to be there, that loved one is going to be on that person's mind. Acknowledge it. Let them know you care.

3) Be there, with no expectations.

As Billy Graham said, the thing we need most during grief is a friend who will stand with us and not leave us. Ultimately, that friend is Jesus. But He has given us, as His followers, the opportunity to stand in for Him, to represent Him to one another. So be there. Even if you don't know what to say. Be there.

Victoria Strong writes:

> Grief is exhausting, bone-tiring. But calls, texts, emails of support matter. Don't get offended if you get no response or if the parents don't want to be social. It isn't personal. Sometimes words need to soak in and linger to be soothing. Sometimes the simple act of responding to outreach feels completely overwhelming. Know your outreach reminds us we

are not alone. That our child is remembered! When you are together, let your friend cry and cry with them. You don't need to be strong for them. (Even in their weakness, they are already stronger than you could ever possibly imagine.) Get comfortable with being uncomfortable and not being able to fully understand. Share empathy – not pity – for what you can imagine. We need you.[21]

Walking with someone through grief is one of the most helpless feelings any of us can have. We just don't feel adequate to the task! But we don't have to leave it to time to make things better. We know the Wounded Healer and, on His behalf, we can walk with one another through the pain.

For further study, see the Discussion Guide for
Chapter 4 on page 135.

− 5 −

CHARITY BEGINS AT HOME

Foreign Aid?

On Tuesday, January 12, 2010, at approximately 4:53 in the afternoon local time, an earthquake struck the southwest part of Haiti. The earthquake measured 7.0 on the Richter scale, and its epicenter was just 16 miles away from Haiti's capital and most populous city, Port-Au-Prince. It is estimated that three million people lived within the area affected by the quake.

The devastation was immense. Haiti's history of impoverishment meant that many of the people affected by the quake lived in substandard housing. The Haitian government estimated that 250,000 residences and 30,000 commercial buildings collapsed or were severely damaged.

Accurate casualty numbers are hard to obtain, and estimates vary widely, but no matter which number you look at, it is terrible.

A University of Michigan study put the death toll, in the first six weeks after the quake, at 160,000. The Haitian government, at the one-year anniversary of the quake, said the death toll was 316,000. Regardless of the actual number, it was overwhelming and it was necessary to bury many of those who died in mass graves.

The international response to the quake was an outpouring of support and financial aid. In the immediate aftermath, the Port-Au-Prince airport became a logistical nightmare as so many planes were attempting to fly supplies in. International governments pledged large sums of money and government and non-government organizations sent large delegations of workers. The United States government alone pledged $906 million dollars and sent a large contingent of military personnel.

In the years following the earthquake, however, questions have been raised as to where exactly all that money went, and who it actually helped. In 2013, three years after the quake, it was reported that only about 1/3 of the $900 million that was promised had actually been spent. Of that $300 million, the largest single recipient was the U.S. government itself, which reimbursed itself for the cost of sending in military personnel. The U.S. also awarded a large amount of money to contractors, only about 2.5% of which went to Haitian companies. Nearly 40% of the money given to contractors, on the other hand, went to companies based in the Washington, D.C. area.

Moreover, one of the biggest "in kind" donations the U.S. made to Haiti were rice and other grains bought at heavily subsidized prices from U.S. suppliers. This made a tidy profit for the American producers, but had the effect of undercutting Haitian farmers.

One of the biggest investments the U.S. made in Haiti following the quake was some $224 million to create an industrial park in the north part of the country, well outside the quake zone. This industrial park is intended to house low-wage garment factories, which will help American retailers sell shoes and apparel at a higher profit margin. Questions have been raised, however, about how much the infusion of jobs is actually helping Haitian residents.[22]

In other words, those who benefitted the most from U.S. aid for one of the worst natural disasters in the Western Hemisphere in the last century were the U.S. military, U.S. contractors, U.S. rice growers, and U.S. big box stores.

I found this story online at TheGuardian.com with a headline that read: "Disaster Aid: How US charity begins at home." And, really, when you think about it, this is pretty much the most literal application of that proverb that you can imagine: making sure that your spending for international aid leads to profits for your own national interests.

A Troubling Phrase

When I first conceived of this book almost 20 years ago, "Charity begins at home" was one of the first phrases I thought of. It's a phrase that has always stuck in my craw.

It probably stems from a church board meeting I was involved in where we were trying to set our missions budget. One of the other board members started to complain that we were spending too much money outside of our organization. His reasoning was that we couldn't be sure how the money we gave away was being spent, or even if the people receiving it really needed it. Besides, he said, wouldn't it be better to spend the money we raised on our own organization? And then he said it: "Doesn't charity begin at home?"

It seems to me, most of the time I hear the phrase, that's the context: we should keep the money we have to meet our needs and the needs of those in our immediate circle before we worry about helping faceless strangers in another community or country. Most of the time I hear the phrase, it is justifying not being generous.

I thought this was going to be an easy phrase to tear apart and tell us all to cut out of our vocabularies. But as I started to dig into it, I discovered this phrase has a lot more going for it than I first gave it credit for. In fact, of all the phrases covered in this book, "Charity begins at home" might just be the closest to expressing a Biblical idea. As we are about to see, when used correctly, this phrase can be very helpful and beautiful.

Putting Your Religion into Practice at Home

Let's start with our usual first question: Is there Biblical truth? Is the idea of charity beginning at home taught in the Bible? The passage we need to look at here is 1 Timothy 5:3–8.

> Give proper recognition to those widows who are really in need. But if a widow has children or grand-children, these should learn first of all to put their religion into practice by caring for their own family and so repaying their parents and grandparents, for this is pleasing to God. The widow who is really in need and left all alone puts her hope in God and continues night and day to pray and to ask God for help. But the widow who lives for pleasure is dead even while she lives. Give the people these instructions, so that no one may be open to blame. Anyone who does not provide for their relatives, and especially for their own household, has denied the faith and is worse than an unbeliever.

This passage is about caring for widows. Now, we need to recognize that widowhood in the world of the Bible was about more than being grief stricken over the death of a husband, as terrible as that is. The time in which the Bible was written was not great for gender equality, to say the least. Women rarely worked outside of the home. They didn't manage property or farm the land. They had very little legal standing in judicial matters. In other words, they had very little economic agency of their own. And so, not only were widowed women in mourning over the death of their husbands, they were also in financial peril.

I'm not saying this was right. It wasn't. And the Bible is actually very progressive in the ways it promotes the rights of women. But that doesn't mean it was easy to be a single, adult female.

Widows are mentioned in the Bible as special recipients of God's love and favor. There are something like 80 references to widows in the Bible. Psalm 68:5 says God is "a father to the fatherless, a defender of widows." Israelites in the Old Testament and Christians in the New Testament are told to have a special charitable concern for widows. That's what this passage in 1 Timothy is about.

But notice, it starts with an interesting phrase. Paul talks about "those widows who are really in need." He's not talking about widows who are especially impoverished, like there is a certain income level they must fall below in order to be considered in need. Rather, the next verse explains what he means. A widow who is really in need is a widow who has no immediate family to support or care for her. These are the widows that the church should go out of its way to help, support, and provide for.

But those widows who have living children and grandchildren? Those widows should not need the church's support because their children and grandchildren should—verse 4—"put their religion into practice by caring for their own family and so repaying their parents and grandparents." A widow with living children should not be in need because those children will step in to take care of her. Children and grandchildren who refuse to provide for these needs—and instead expect the church to do so—are denying their duty and displeasing God.

Verse 5, then, goes back to the widow who has no such immediate family. She is the widow who is really in need, and thus she is dependent on God to provide. By extension, Paul is saying that she is the one the church should care for.

Verse 8, then, wraps up this paragraph with a general principle: "Anyone who does not provide for their relatives, and especially for their own household, has denied the faith and is worse than an unbeliever."

Here is where we can see the Biblical foundation for the phrase "charity begins at home." What business do we have caring for orphans and widows across the globe, or even right across the street, if we do not provide for the relatives in our own homes? In fact, Paul says, even people who do not believe in Jesus know enough to care for their own relatives. If Christians refuse to care for their own family, they are denying the faith.

Jesus makes a very similar point in Matthew 15 when He takes the Pharisees to task for some of their small-print religious rules. Apparently the Pharisees had invented a rule that said any property you devoted to God was set apart and thus not subject to any other law. And so they made a big deal out of saying this or that property was dedicated to God—even while they continued to use it—and thus they were unable to use it to care for their elderly parents. Jesus puts it like this:

> For God said, "Honor your father and mother" and "Anyone who curses their father or mother is to be put to death." But you say that if anyone declares that what might have been used to help their father or mother is "devoted to God," they are not to 'honor their father or mother' with it. Thus you nullify the

word of God for the sake of your tradition. You
hypocrites! (Matthew 15:4–7)

Neglecting your own family out of some sort of religious devotion
does not impress Jesus. I take this to mean that giving generously
to missions and charities while your own immediate family is
uncared for is not seen as an act of selfless worship, but as an act of
selfish hypocrisy.

The Bible definitely teaches that we have an obligation to
provide for our own families. We can argue if that kind of help fits
into the modern definition of the word "charity," but in this sense
"Charity begins at home" is a Biblical idea.

If Charity Begins at Home, Does it Stop There Also?

Now, let's turn to the second question: What's wrong with this
phrase? Even though the phrase "Charity begins at home" is not a
strict Bible quote, we can see where the idea is taught in the Bible.
Is there anything wrong, then, with us using this phrase?

Here's where I want to go back to the context in which I so
often hear the phrase uttered. In my experience, the problem
comes when we use this phrase to justify our decision to not be
charitable outside of our homes. When we use the phrase "Charity
begins at home," we are often implying that it ends there as well.
The impression is that, because our need to provide for our own is
so great, we couldn't possibly afford to give to anyone else.

I see at least three things wrong with this kind of thinking:

1. It is selfish.
In Philippians 2:3–4 it says: "Do nothing out of selfish ambition or
vain conceit. Rather, in humility value others above your-

selves, not looking to your own interests but each of you to the interests of the others."

Let's face it. When we use this phrase to justify a decision to not support a cause or a need, what we are really saying is that we would rather spend the money on ourselves than on someone else. More often than not, it is not because we have a widowed mother to care for or a new foster child to provide for, but because we are hoping to buy a new TV for the den or want to go out for dinner on Friday night.

We also need to be careful about creating a false equivalence between our personal wants and the needs of the poor. There is a qualitative difference between many of the wants and needs of the average American family and that of the average Haitian family. That doesn't necessarily mean that we need to impoverish ourselves to the same level as a Haitian family in an effort to improve their situation, but it certainly shows the superficiality of saying that "Charity begins at home."

2. It treats compassion as a zero-sum game.

A zero-sum game implies that if I win, you have to lose. It implies that the scales must always be in balance.

When I use the phrase "Charity begins at home" to justify a decision not to give money, I am implying that if I show concern in one area, I have that much less concern to show in another area. It treats compassion like a finite resource. But compassion should not be a finite resource. Just because I care about one issue—like, say, feeding hungry school children in America—that doesn't mean I cannot also care about another issue—like, say, feeding hungry school children in Haiti. We need to stop assuming that standing up for one cause means we don't care about any others.

1 Thessalonians 3:12 says: "May the Lord make your love increase and overflow for each other and for everyone else, just as

ours does for you." When you start to show love, you find it is something that never runs out.

3. It creates a "leftover" mindset for our giving.

The other big problem I see with the way we so often use the phrase "Charity begins at home" is that it leaves us thinking that we give away what is left over after everything else is paid for. Under this mindset, we tell ourselves that first we'll pay the mortgage or rent, then we'll buy groceries, then we'll make the car payment, then we'll buy some clothes for the kids, then we'll buy something nice for ourselves, then we'll put some money in savings, then we'll go out for a little entertainment, and then, and only then, if there is anything left over, we'll give some money to the church or to charity.

One of the main problems with this mindset is that when we reach the end of the month, we often find there is very little money left over.

This is one of the reasons the Bible uses the concept of first-fruits when it talks about giving. Proverbs 3:9 says: "Honor the Lord with your wealth, with the firstfruits of all your crops."

The idea is that we should make our giving plan first, and fit all of our other obligations and goals around that plan. Similarly, when it comes to our volunteer time or other involvement in charity, if we only wait until we have free time to get involved, we might just find it never happens.

Using the phrase "Charity begins at home" does not justify bringing our leftovers to God.

Looking Out for the Stranger

Now, third question: Is there better news in the gospel? Does the Bible give us a better way to think about charity?

The gospel story, of course, is all about the selflessness of Jesus in giving up His privileges as the Son of God in order to sacrifice Himself for us. He did this, not just for His immediate circle of family, but for love of the whole world. In fact, in the Philippians passage I quoted earlier about doing nothing out of selfish ambition, when the Apostle Paul needs an illustration of what that looks like, he tells the story of Jesus, who, though He was in very nature God, made himself nothing and took on the nature of a servant. (Phil. 2:5–11)

2 Corinthians 8:9 contains one of the best summaries of the good news of Jesus in a single verse. And it frames it in terms of giving and sacrifice: "For you know the grace of our Lord Jesus Christ, that though he was rich, yet for your sake he became poor, so that you through his poverty might become rich."

The good news of the gospel is the story of Jesus sacrificing for us. And thus, as those who follow Him, those who are called by His name, we are also called to sacrifice. Not just for those within our own home, but also for those in need both near and far.

Here are some Bible verses which call us to have compassion, even for those we do not know. Proverbs 19:17: "Whoever is kind to the poor lends to the Lord, and he will reward them for what they have done."

Isaiah 58:6–7, 10:

> Is not this the kind of fasting I have chosen:
> to loose the chains of injustice
>   and untie the cords of the yoke,
> to set the oppressed free
>   and break every yoke?
> Is it not to share your food with the hungry
>   and to provide the poor wanderer with shelter—
> when you see the naked, to clothe them,

and not to turn away from your own flesh and blood?
...
and if you spend yourselves in behalf of the hungry
    and satisfy the needs of the oppressed,
then your light will rise in the darkness,
    and your night will become like the noonday.

And Matthew 25:37–40:

"Then the righteous will answer him, 'Lord, when did we see you hungry and feed you, or thirsty and give you something to drink? When did we see you a stranger and invite you in, or needing clothes and clothe you? When did we see you sick or in prison and go to visit you?'

"The King will reply, 'Truly I tell you, whatever you did for one of the least of these brothers and sisters of mine, you did for me.'"

As Christians, we are called to be involved in charity that is far-reaching and generous. Just as Jesus sacrificed a great deal for us, so we are called to be sacrificial in our care for the poor, the hungry, the oppressed, and the stranger.

Learning to Love

Finally, let's go back to the phrase itself, "Charity begins at home." We can see that there is Biblical backing for the idea that Christians have a moral and ethical obligation to care for their own families. We can also see that the way we often use the phrase—as a justification for not being generous—runs counter to the gospel of Jesus.

But let's look a little more carefully at the phrase and consider if we really understand what it is saying. As I researched it, I learned that a good case can be made that the phrase does not mean that home is the place where our resources should first be spent, so much as home is the place where charity should be learned. In other words, "Charity begins at home" means that the practice of charity is first learned in the home.

Part of the confusion stems from the fact that the meaning of the word "charity" has shifted over time. This proverb, in English, is actually quite old, and can be traced back to the days before Shakespeare. You may be aware that in the King James Version of the Bible—which comes from Shakespearian times—the preferred translation for the word "*agape,*" which describes God's love, is "charity." Thus, in the KJV, the Bible's famous love chapter, 1 Corinthians 13, is all about "charity." "Faith, hope and charity... But the greatest of these is charity." More than a word that describes giving to the poor, it is a word that describes selfless acts of love.

With that in mind, a better way of expressing what this proverb originally meant would be "love begins at home." That ideally means we learn love—and the practice of charitable giving—within our families, so we can exercise it with others outside of the home.

The point being, when people first started saying "Charity begins at home," what they were trying to get across was that being a loving person in the home leads to being a loving person out in the world. It's really an instruction about how to be more generous, which is kind of the opposite of the way it's used today as a warning *against* being too generous.

This leads to two brief points of application.

1. Be generous in your family.

The home is the first place where we should be generous and giving. As tempting as it might be to say that we must pinch pennies at every point in order to give more away, there is something to be said for being liberal with our spouse and children and grandchildren. This is not the same as saying we should indulge our personal comforts, but rather that we should forgo them for the sake of demonstrating care and concern and love for our family.

One way we demonstrate the lavish and generous love of God our Father is by showing lavish and generous love to our children. One of the best ways for them to learn about His generous love for them is when they see it in their parents. Generosity with our kids is one of the main ways we can create kids who are generous.

David Mathis writes:

> In our sin, we're prone to cut ourselves financial slack while tightening the purse strings on others, sometimes especially those in our own household. But the gospel turns that on its head. When funds are limited, our inclinations should be to deprive ourselves in order to be generous toward others, especially those under our own roof.[23]

2. Teach your family to be generous.

If the meaning of the phrase "Charity begins at home" is that charity is learned at home, then we must teach our children to be generous. Volunteer. Get them to volunteer. Find charities you want to support financially and let them know you are doing it. Find a way they can contribute as well. Bring cookies to an ailing neighbor and bring your kids along. Talk about your family plan for giving and explain to them why you do it.

Randy Alcorn writes:

> We should be raising up a generation of givers, not keepers. But the next generation is growing up

amid—and inheriting—vast wealth. They have no tradition of giving, no vision for investing in eternity, no sense that God's purpose for prospering them is not so they can live in luxury, but so they can help their churches, aid the poor, and reach the lost.[24]

Charity begins at home. That doesn't mean spend only on yourself and those closest to you. It means that the practice of charity, and the mindset of generosity, is only going to happen if it is learned in our homes first.

For further study, see the Discussion Guide for Chapter 5 on page 138.

— 6 —

JUST FOLLOW YOUR HEART

The Book of Hezekiah

During my annual week at Bible Camp when I was around 11 years old, I had a counselor I thought was pretty cool. I don't remember his name, but I'm pretty sure he was a college student at an area Christian college. And one of the things that really impressed me about him was his knowledge of the Bible.

In fact, one of the things he did a lot was when someone would say something interesting or profound, he'd say, "That's in the book of Hezekiah. Hezekiah 3:15." He did that repeatedly throughout the week. Sometimes he'd even quote verses and then tell us that they were from the book of Hezekiah. Hezekiah 2:21. Hezekiah 8, verses 6 and 7.

It wasn't until toward the end of the week, when one of us actually tried to look Hezekiah up in our own Bible, that we figured it out. There is no book of Hezekiah. Hezekiah is a character in the Bible—he's actually a king of Judah that gets mentioned fairly often in the Old Testament—but there is no book named after him. It was then that our counselor explained to us what he was doing.

He said that he had learned it in a Bible class at college. The professor had talked about the many ideas and sayings that people think are in the Bible, but are not. He liked to assign these fictional Bible verses to a fictional book of the Bible. Hezekiah. And my counselor and some of his buddies thought that was so much fun that they started doing it as well.

I don't know why exactly—maybe it was a little foreshadowing of the preacher I would become—but I thought that was one of the coolest things ever. The book of Hezekiah. Hezekiah 12:22.

The Song of Disney

One of the things I've discovered as I've worked on this book is that there is a small corner of the internet that is devoted to books like Hezekiah. That is, I've found blog posts about some of these clichés that often assign them fictional Bible locations. I've seen sayings attributed to *Hezekiah*. Fictional verses from *Phillips 66*. A book of *Hesitations*. Made up verses from *1st and 2nd Oprah*. And a *Song of Disney*.

And it's that last one that I want to talk about now. If our saying for this chapter had a quasi-Biblical citation, it would have to be Song of Disney 1:1.

The saying is "Just follow your heart."

I don't mean to offend anyone, but I might. I'm going to talk about beloved children's movies, and not everything I say will be nice. I'm going to challenge the worldview of the Magic Kingdom.

Before I do, let me say that, for the most part, I like Disney movies. My first date with my wife Beth was to see Disney's "Beauty and the Beast." I appreciate that there is a movie studio out there producing enjoyable movies that are not dependent on gratuitous violence or sex or profanity. And most of Disney's movies have positive themes like friendship, courage, and sacrifice. Disney movies also teach our children that they don't always have to come from a special place in order to do special things.

But one of the overriding themes of many Disney movies—and one which ties into a sentiment that is prevalent in our society—can be summarized in the phrase "Just follow your heart." It's the notion that inside of us is a moral compass whose arrow always points to True North, and if we just listen to our hearts and follow our dreams and believe in ourselves enough, we'll always know the right things to do and the things we do will always be right.

There are many examples. Cinderella sings a song called "A Dream is a Wish Your Heart Makes" that says if you believe in your dreams hard enough and long enough, eventually they will come true. The plot to "Frozen" turns on its main song "Let It Go" when Princess Elsa accepts who she is and finally forgets about society's rules and expectations for her. Jiminy Cricket sings "When You Wish Upon a Star" to Pinocchio and assures him that anything his heart desires will come true. The Disney company liked that one so much they made it their theme song.

"Just follow your heart" is the worldview of Disney, but it is not the worldview of the Bible. And yet, it is a phrase that will often creep into Christian circles. We should consider it critically. Just because it gets repeated so often does not mean it is good advice.

Alignment

First question: Is there Biblical truth? Is there any part of this phrase that matches up to Biblical teaching? And the short answer is, "No."

But if we want to be generous, we might point to the second half of Psalm 37:4: "...and he will give you the desires of your heart."

That sounds pretty close to "just follow your heart." In fact, this line matches up very closely to the line from Pinocchio.

It wouldn't even be unusual for you to talk with another Christian who might reference Psalm 37:4 to tell you that God wants to give them their heart's desire. This sounds like a promise from God to give you whatever you want. But we have read the first half of the verse. It's not a good idea to take Bible verses out of their context. The whole of Psalm 37:4 says, "Take delight in the Lord, and he will give you the desires of your heart."

That's an important precondition. We are promised that God will grant the desires of our hearts when we "take delight in the Lord." The verse before says that we should "trust in the Lord and do good." The idea is that as we take pleasure in learning more about God and following His will, God will more and more shape the desires of our hearts to conform to the things He wants.

Instead of a suggestion that the desires of our heart are always good and God will give us whatever we desire, this verse is a call for us to move our heart toward God so that the things we desire look like the things He wants to accomplish. The more we find our joy and delight in the goodness of God, the more our desires will move away from our self-centered wants and be replaced by a yearning to experience God's will and purpose in our lives.

This idea is key for this chapter, and we'll come back to it later. But for now, I want to show you that this isn't the only place where the Bible speaks like this. Consider Proverbs 19:21: "Many are the plans in a person's heart, but it is the Lord's purpose that prevails."

Our hearts are not life's infallible guides, but the Lord's purpose is.

Also, Proverbs 16:9: "In their hearts humans plan their course, but the Lord establishes their steps."

And then, from the New Testament, Romans 12:2. Rather than use the New International translation of this verse, let me share with you the New International Readers Version. It helps us get the sense a little easier.

> Don't live the way this world lives. Let your way of thinking be completely changed. Then you will be able to test what God wants for you. And you will agree that what he wants is right. His plan is good and pleasing and perfect.

The point is, when we let our way of thinking be changed—that is, when we conform our hearts to the heart of God—then we will agree that what God wants is what is right. We are not supposed to follow our hearts so much as we are supposed to let our hearts be transformed to reflect the good, pleasing, and perfect plan of God.

All of which is to say, "Just follow your heart" does not contain much Biblical truth. In fact, the Bible teaches something that is almost completely the opposite.

Lies, Desensitization, and Arrogance

Let's go now to the second question: What's wrong with it? Where does this statement go wrong? I have three answers to this question.

1. The heart is a liar.
It's a bad idea to follow our heart, because it has a tendency to steer us wrong. Jeremiah 17:9 says, "The heart is deceitful above all things and beyond cure. Who can understand it?"

This is not a very encouraging verse. But it is in keeping with the Biblical view of the sinful nature of humanity. Our hearts tend to be selfish, self-centered, and on the lookout for the path that will lead to the greatest pleasure for ourselves. And so, our hearts have a tendency to lie to us. They have a tendency to tell us to pursue paths that are not always right, best, or good, but which appeal to our sinful natures.

One of the reasons we don't always notice the bad advice when Disney characters are told to just follow their hearts is because the heroes in those movies tend to make the good and right and heroic choices. Their hearts tell them to do the right thing. But that's not real life.

Jon Bloom has written a book called *Don't Follow Your Heart*. In it he writes:

> The truth is, no one lies to us more than our own hearts. No one. If our hearts are compasses, they are Jack Sparrow compasses. They don't tell us the truth; they just tell us what we want.... They are not benevolent; they are pathologically selfish. In fact, if we do what our hearts tell us to do, we will pervert and impoverish every desire, every beauty, every person, every wonder, and every joy. Our hearts want to consume these things for our own self-glory and self-indulgence.[25]

For a Biblical example, he points to David. David is described in the Bible as a man after God's own heart (Acts 13:22). And, in fact, when he followed God's own heart, he did very well. He established the kingdom of Israel, wrote most of the book of Psalms, established the family lineage of Jesus.

But there are times in David's life when he followed his own heart, and the results were disastrous. When David followed his heart into an affair with Bathsheba, he robbed her of her chastity, ended up robbing her husband Uriah of his life, and brought on a pattern of family dysfunction that almost cost him his kingdom and resulted in the death of his son Absalom.

How many of us can think of examples of financial disasters that have resulted when someone has followed his or her heart into a terrible business decision? Or marriages that have been wrecked when a spouse followed his or her heart into an affair? Or lives that have been destroyed when someone has followed his or her heart into an addiction? The heart is a liar. It does not always give us the best advice.

2. Culture has a deceptive magnetic pull.

It's a bad idea to always follow our hearts because our hearts are affected by our culture in ways we may not always realize.

One of my favorite passages of scripture is the beginning of Isaiah 6 where Isaiah enters the temple and has a vision of God seated on his throne with angels surrounding him and calling "Holy, Holy, Holy." I love the passage because of the awe-inspiring and glorious picture it presents of God.

But it is also interesting because of Isaiah's reaction to being in the presence of the Holy God. Isaiah 6:5 shares it: "'Woe to me!' I cried. 'I am ruined! For I am a man of unclean lips, and I live among a people of unclean lips, and my eyes have seen the King, the Lord Almighty.'"

Not only is Isaiah aware of his own sinfulness, he is also acutely aware of the sinfulness of his people. I take that to mean, in part, that Isaiah lives in a culture that has moved away from God so much so that there may be things that he does and believes that are so normative to his culture that he is not even aware that they are sinful. Isaiah is admitting that he is guilty of sins he doesn't even know about, because they are a normal part of the place he lives.

And that is one of the constant battles a Christian must fight. There are so many things—cultural beliefs, popular trends, conventional wisdom—that are such an ingrained part of our society that, even though they might not square up with the Bible, we tend to take them as accepted truth. If our hearts do carry a moral compass, we sometimes have a hard time recognizing how the needle is being pulled off-center by the magnetic power of our culture.

That's why we need to think critically about the lessons our culture teaches us. The idea that everybody has their own truth, the notion that every religion leads to the same ultimate place, the idea that moral choices are all relative...these are all ideas that can lead our hearts down some strange paths.

3. We answer to a higher authority.

It's a bad idea to just follow our hearts because our hearts do not get the final say. Consider this verse from 1 Corinthians 4:3–4: "I care very little if I am judged by you or by any human court; indeed, I do not even judge myself. My conscience is clear, but that does not make me innocent. It is the Lord who judges me."

Paul is defending himself against critics who say he should not be an apostle. The details of that dispute are not important to us now, but notice what Paul says about his conscience. He says that he has checked his heart, and everything he has done has fit with his heart. His conscience is clear. He doesn't feel like, or believe, that he has done anything wrong.

But then notice what he says, "that does not make me innocent." Paul gets that just because he believes his motives are pure, that doesn't necessarily mean they were. He understands his heart may have led him astray. Ultimately, he says, the one who will judge Him is the Lord.

That reminds me of another phrase that is out there, but is not really Biblical. I've heard people say, "Only God can judge me." I believe it is popular as a tattoo. It's the name of a rap song by Tupac. And the impression I get, when I hear people say it, is that as long as they are true to themselves and have a clear conscience, then all their critics should be silent because it is between them and God. In other words, it's just another way of saying that they set their own rules for life.

But that is pretty much the opposite of what Paul is expressing here. He is admitting, up front, that his conscience can be a faulty guide. He is not claiming that his heart is the final authority, but that he needs to submit himself to the Lord's will.

If you truly believe that the best solution to every decision you must make is to "just follow your heart," then you have set up your heart (and yourself) as a higher authority than God.

Let God Lead Your Heart

Finally, let's ask the third question: Is there better news in the gospel? Does the Bible have better advice for us than to follow our lying, arrogant hearts? Of course, it does. I have three things to say here as well.

1. Trust the God who changes hearts.

That verse from Jeremiah 17:9 is pretty grim. The heart is deceptive above all things. It is beyond cure. Who can understand it? Basically, from a human perspective, our hearts are unfixable. From a human perspective, we should never, never, ever, ever trust our hearts, or anybody else's.

But God is in the business of changing human hearts. What is impossible for us is not impossible for God. In Romans 6:17–18 it says this:

> But thanks be to God that, though you used to be
> slaves to sin, you have come to obey from your heart
> the pattern of teaching that has now claimed your

allegiance. You have been set free from sin and have become slaves to righteousness.

God can take out your heart of stone and put in a heart of flesh (Ezekiel 36:26). That's part of the miracle of salvation Jesus won for us at the cross and the empty grave.

The first thing we need to do, if we don't want our hearts to continue to lead us astray, is surrender them to Jesus. Admit that we are not the final authority in our lives, but He is. Allow Him to do some heart surgery and send the Holy Spirit to start giving us better advice.

But, even when we do surrender to Jesus, that doesn't mean our hearts are always going to be right. As long as we are still alive on this earth, there will be parts of our old nature, and the influences of our fallen culture, still influencing our lives. The second thing we need to do is:

2. Lead our hearts.

Instead of following the wishes and desires of our hearts, we need to learn to train our hearts to wish for and desire the correct things. Colossians 3:1–2 says, "Since, then, you have been raised with Christ, set your hearts on things above, where Christ is, seated at the right hand of God. Set your minds on things above, not on earthly things."

The key is to set our hearts on the things of God. That's the point Jesus is making in the Sermon on the Mount when he says, "where your treasure is, there will your heart be also" (Matthew 6:21). The idea is that our hearts are going to move toward whatever we treasure most, and so we must make a point to treasure God most, so that we can lead our hearts towards Him.

It's the same idea we saw in Psalm 37:4. When we find our delight in the Lord, then he will give us what our hearts desire, which is Himself. It's the point of Romans 12:2. When we transform our hearts and minds, then we start to see how good and right and pleasing God's will is for us.

It is only when we lead our hearts to focus on things above that we can really trust our hearts to take us where we belong.

3. We must follow Jesus.

Ultimately, it is not our hearts that we should follow, but our Savior. He is the good shepherd who guides us in paths of righteousness (Psalm 23:3). The sheep who recognize and listen to His voice will be led to life (John 10:27 and John 14:6).

Jon Bloom writes:

> [T]though your heart will try to shepherd you today, do not follow it. It is not a shepherd. It is a pompous sheep that, due to remaining sin, has some wolf-like qualities. Don't follow it, and be careful even listening to it. Remember, your heart only tells you what you want, not where you should go. So, only listen to it to note what it's telling you about what you want, and then take your wants, both good and evil, to Jesus...[26]

Don't follow your heart. Follow Jesus.

For further study, see the Discussion Guide for Chapter 6 on page 141.

66

– 7 –

GOD WILL NOT GIVE YOU MORE THAN YOU CAN HANDLE

That's Not How I Remember It

In 1991, Kevin Costner starred in a movie titled "Robin Hood: Prince of Thieves." Today the movie is probably best remembered for its soundtrack and the love song "(Everything I Do) I Do It For You" by Bryan Adams. I remember it as a pretty good action-adventure movie that I saw during my first summer of college. It's also a movie my wife Beth and I re-watched together on video tape (VCR's were so cool!) while we were dating.

One of the most memorable parts of the movie, for me, involved Alan Rickman, the actor who played an over-the-top bad guy as the Sheriff of Nottingham. At one point, after Robin Hood has once again bested him, the Sheriff rants to his underlings that once he captures Robin Hood he's going to "cut his heart out with a spoon!" At this, one of his dimwitted deputies replies in confusion, "A spoon, why a spoon?" To which the exasperated Sheriff says, "Because it will hurt more you idiot!"

For some reason, that scene tickled me. And so, for the last 20 years or so, whenever Beth and I are cooking together and one of us asks the other one to grab a spoon, we'll say to each other, "A spoon, why a spoon?" To which the other will reply, "Because it will hurt more you idiot!" As you can imagine, this has provided us with lots of laughs over the years.

So imagine our disappointment a few years ago when Beth found a DVD of the movie in the bargain bin and brought it home. For one thing, the DVD was so old that you actually had to stop midway through the movie and flip the DVD over to play the second half. For another, the movie really hasn't held up that well. We thought it was cheesy and dated. But the worst part was, when we got to our favorite scene, we found out we'd been misquoting it. What the deputy actually says after the Sheriff threatens to cut Robin Hood's heart out with a spoon is, "Why a spoon, cousin? Why not an axe?" To which the Sheriff replies, "Because it's DULL, you twit. It'll hurt more."

Personally, I prefer our version of the quote, but that's not quite how it goes.

Did you know that some of the movie lines we repeat most often are often quoted wrong? Here are a few examples:

- From "Apollo 13," the line we usually quote is, "Houston, we have a problem." But the actual movie line is, "...Ah, Houston, we've had a problem."
- From "Field of Dreams" we usually quote, "If you build it, they will come." But, as it turns out, the actual quote is slightly different: "If you build it, he will come."

- From "Casablanca" we love to quote Bogart, "Play it again, Sam." But the actual line of movie dialogue is, "Play it, Sam. Play 'As Time Goes By.'"
- From "Star Wars: The Empire Strikes Back" who hasn't done their best Darth Vader voice, "Luke, I am your father!"? But it really goes, "No, I am your father."

In the long run, it's not that big of a deal. Most of the misquotes don't change the meaning all that much. It's just changing a word or two, and often it makes the quote easier to repeat in multiple settings. And, who really cares, it's just the movies, right?

But what about when we do the same thing with scripture? What about when we start misquoting scripture? Do we remember the Bible saying things it really doesn't say?

I'm not talking about switching a word or two, like saying, "In the beginning God *made* the heavens and the earth" instead of "In the beginning God *created* the heavens and the earth." Different translations will often vary in word choice and word order.

I'm talking about when we misremember what a verse says in such a way that we change the very meaning of that verse. The cliché in this chapter is one of those verses. It's a line that really is found in the Bible, but not in the way most of us think.

1 Corinthians 10:13

The verse is 1 Corinthians 10:13. Here's how the New International Version puts it: "And God is faithful; he will not let you be tempted beyond what you can bear."

It's a good verse. An important verse. But a lot of us have summarized that quote—and changed it around to make it a little more memorable—to say, "God will not give you more than you can handle."

It's a common saying. One I am sure you have heard. Probably one you have repeated from time to time. You can see how it sounds similar to 1 Corinthians 10:13. But it is a misquote. And, in this case, I am afraid that it is a misquote that does more harm than good.

This cliché is a little different from others in this book. Not only is it a close approximation of an actual Bible verse many of us have repeated, I think it might also be one that many of us truly believe. It sounds like Biblical teaching that we've heard often.

More than that, it is something we want to be true. "God won't give me more than I can handle." We tell ourselves that as we face something difficult. We want to believe it. This chapter might even sound like I am challenging one of your core convictions.

If that is the case, I hope you'll hang in there with me. I'm not saying this statement is completely wrong, but I am saying that we need to look carefully at it. And, as we'll see, there are some implications of this saying that are not at all helpful.

What Happens in Corinth

Let's begin by looking for the Biblical truth. As we've already seen, "God will not give you more than you can handle" sounds like a pretty close approximation of 1 Corinthians 10:13. Let's look a little bit more closely at the whole verse:

> No temptation has overtaken you except what is common to mankind. And God is faithful; he will not let you be tempted beyond what you can bear. But when you are tempted, he will also provide a way out so that you can endure it.

You can see how we might get "God will not give you more than you can handle" out of this verse. In fact, many of our English translations have a footnote by the word "tempted" that tells us the original Greek word could also be translated as "tested."

The verse seems to be saying that no matter what comes our way—whether it's a temptation or a trial or a bit of suffering or a time of tragedy—we can take comfort from the fact that God is not going to overload us. He won't allow us to be tested beyond what we can bear. He won't give us more than we can handle.

It's a hopeful idea. It's easy to understand why we say this phrase to one another. When someone is experiencing a particularly bad stretch, when they have received a succession of bad news, we say to them, "Hang in there. I know it's rough right now, but God won't give you more than you can handle. There is an end point. He's going to provide a way out so that you can endure it. You can get through this."

It's the "light at the end of the tunnel" approach. It's the promise that things won't get so bad that they become utterly hopeless.

That looks and sounds biblical, right? This seems like a good application of God's Word.

When we look a little more closely at the verse and its context, however, we will see that there is a reason most of the English translations use the word "temptation" and not "testing" here.

This passage is part of a letter written by Paul to the church in the Greek city of Corinth. Corinth was a large port city, and Paul started the church there around A.D. 51. Like many port cities, Corinth had a cosmopolitan and international feel. There were pagan shrines and different religious expressions everywhere. In fact, sacrifice at pagan temples was big business. If meat was purchased in the local marketplace, chances were good that it came from an animal that had been sacrificed to a pagan god.

More than that, Corinth was known for being a very permissive place. In the Roman world they had a saying, "to live like a

Corinthian," which was a code for drunkenness and partying. It was sort of the Roman world equivalent of "what happens in Vegas."

Most of the Christians Paul was writing to had come out of this world and they still lived in the midst of this world. And so, now, as followers of Christ, they were trying to live differently. They no longer wanted to get caught up in the idol worship or temple rituals they had left behind. They didn't want to participate in the sexual immorality that was involved in the worship of Aphrodite, the Greek goddess of love.

But it was all around them. It was constantly in their face. They couldn't buy meat without feeling like they were participating in pagan worship. They couldn't walk down the street without being propositioned by one of Aphrodite's temple servants.

That's the context for this verse. Paul is specifically trying to help them stand up in the face of temptation. He's warning them not to let down their guard, not to think they are above all this temptation. But he's also encouraging them that they have the resources to avoid falling into these old patterns of sin. God is faithful! God is not going to let any temptation come their way that they cannot stand up under. It is not inevitable that they will go back to their old way of life.

The verse really is about temptation, and it is incredibly encouraging! When you are tempted to fall into some old habit, when that old pattern of sin that you thought would go away once you gave your life to Jesus starts to creep back in, take heart! You are not helpless against temptation. You can stand up to it, God will provide a way out! God will not let you be tempted beyond what you can bear.

In that way, the phrase "God will not give you more than you can handle" does ring true. As a follower of Christ, you are not a helpless victim of sin.

Errors

But if we are using this verse to tell someone that God will not give them more suffering than they can handle, we may be asking the verse to say more than it really does. Let's ask: Where does "God will not give us more than we can handle" run counter to Biblical teaching?

1. A mistaken expectation of fairness.
Think of it this way. Imagine that you are moving and you have two children. One is a strapping sixteen-year-old football player who is dedicated to getting into the weight room, and the other is a two-year-old toddler who has just figured out how to walk. Now, let's say both are eager to help you move your stuff into the new house and you are standing at the bed of the pick-up distributing the boxes. How are you going to do it? You're going to give the heavy stuff to the sixteen-year-old, right? And you're going to give the light stuff to the toddler. Like, you're going to give a heavy box of books to the 16-year-old, and you're going to open up the box and give one book to the toddler. You don't want to give the little one more than she can handle.

Well, instinctively, I think that's what we have in mind when we say that God will not give us more than we can handle. We assume that God is making some sort of evaluation about how strong we are and then assigning our trials accordingly. We like the idea that there must be some sort of cosmic scale, and God is measuring out our assignments in a way that measures up to our strength.

You are not going to overload your child's arms and then watch them crash to the ground with stuff splayed everywhere. That wouldn't be fair. We assume God works the same way.

But, here's the thing. There's nothing in the Bible that says God is fair in this way.

In fact, God is decidedly unfair, and it's a good thing. He doesn't deal with us as our sins deserve. He is longsuffering, forbearing, gracious, and abounding in love.

If He were absolutely fair, none of us would be able to draw our next breath. More than that, God causes the sun to shine and the rain to fall on both the righteous and the unrighteous (Matthew 5:45).

Mitch Chase says, "God transcends the categories of fair and unfair to such a degree that we have no position to evaluate his actions or weigh his will. His ways aren't subject to our culture's standard of fairness."[27]

God's unfairness can be a good thing.

But, at the same time, we still live in a fallen world, and this fallen world is not fair either. I've heard Andy Stanley say in one of his sermons, "Fairness died in the Garden of Eden," and it's true. Because of the fallen nature of our world, suffering comes in ways that are not predictable or fair. Some people live in mansions and seem to have success with whatever they do, while others die in the horrors of third-world slums.

Suffering does not get measured out in ways that are rational or fair. And there is no Biblical promise of a cosmic scale that will distribute suffering in a balanced way.

2. The implication that enduring suffering is about our strength.

When we say "God won't give you more than you can handle," we're saying to that person that they are strong enough to get through this. They are tough. They are fighters.

In fact, the statement is a sort of backhanded compliment. We're saying something like, "God must really think you are something to give you such hard trials." There's even a famous quote attributed to Mother Theresa along these lines. She says, "I know that God won't give me more trouble than I can handle ... but sometimes I wish he wouldn't trust me so much."

It's almost a humble brag. It's a way of saying, "Boy, things are tough for me now...my circumstances are awful... but you know God wouldn't give me all this junk if He didn't think I could handle it."

I learned a new phrase as I was writing this chapter. There are whole Pinterest pages dedicated to it. It exists as bumper stickers and wall hangings. It goes, "God gives His hardest battles to His strongest soldiers."

Again, I can see how all this can help you get through tough times. Sometimes you need a little pep talk that says you are tough enough, strong enough, and resilient enough to survive even the most heartbreaking of tragedies. It's nice to think that God believes in you enough to allow you to go through something like that.

But there's a problem with this. At the point of tragedy, when we feel most down and depleted, this Christianism is pointing us inward and telling us to find our strength in ourselves. This is really just a self-help message dressed up in God language. Instead of directing us to find our strength in Jesus, this proverb just tells us to dig deeper inside ourselves.

And if we find that we can't dig any deeper, then what?

3. Counter Examples in Scripture.

The truth is, you can find story after story of people in the Bible who were given far more than they could handle.

Take David. After his sin with Bathsheba and the family tragedies that followed it, David found that he'd come to the end of his rope. In Psalm 38:4 and 8, he says,

> My guilt has overwhelmed me
>   like a burden too heavy to bear.
>
>   ...

> My guilt has overwhelmed me
> like a burden too heavy to bear.

And what about Job?

You say to me, "Ah, Russell, doesn't Job prove you wrong? Isn't the whole point of Job that he was strong enough to handle whatever came his way? Wasn't that the whole point of the bet between Satan and God?"

But that's not the question that Job seeks to answer. It wasn't whether Job was strong enough. The question was whether he would continue to trust God even if his suffering became too much to bear.

And it did become too much to bear. In Job 3:26, Job says, "I have no peace, no quietness; I have no rest, but only turmoil."

And then there is the example of Jesus Himself. The night before the cross, in the Garden of Gethsemane, Jesus found that the cup of wrath He was about to drink was too awful to contemplate. Mark 14:33–34 shares, "He took Peter, James and John along with him, and he began to be deeply distressed and troubled. 'My soul is overwhelmed with sorrow to the point of death.'"

There are all kinds of examples in scripture of people who face suffering far beyond their ability to handle. In fact, it rarely appears that a person's strength or "ability to handle" things is the determining factor in God's decision to call them. As cool as it sounds to say that "God gives his hardest battles to his strongest soldiers," the reality seems to be the opposite:

- Moses, who had the assignment of leading God's people out of slavery, made excuses and tried to hide behind his stutter.
- Gideon, who led the fight against the Midianites, was a coward that God found hiding in a wine press.

- Mary, who had the privilege of bringing Jesus into the world, was a peasant girl barely into her teens.

God doesn't always look for the toughest or strongest, but He seems to delight in using those the world tends to overlook. As Paul says to the Corinthians, God likes to use the weak things of the world to shame the strong (1 Corinthians 1:27). He hides his treasure in jars of clay to show that the strength at work comes not from us, but from Him (2 Corinthians 4:7).

Rely On God

Which leads directly to our third question: Is there better news in the gospel?

Instead of going through life believing God will never give us more than we can handle, can we actually find better news in the notion that sometimes God will allow us to face trials beyond our ability to bear? I think so.

In 2 Corinthians 1:8–9, Paul writes,

> We do not want you to be uninformed, brothers and sisters, about the troubles we experienced in the province of Asia. We were under great pressure, far beyond our ability to endure, so that we despaired of life itself. Indeed, we felt we had received the sentence of death.

Here is another example of God allowing someone to face problems beyond their strength. This is Paul, the same person who wrote that God will not let you be tempted beyond what you can bear—writing to the same people, in fact—now saying that he was under great pressure, far beyond his ability to endure.

We're not sure exactly which incident in his life this verse is referring to—there were many—but Paul tells us that he believed he was going to die. He despaired of life itself. This was far more than he could handle.

Then he provides a crucial insight into his despair. Why were he and his companions given more than they could handle? The last phrase in verse 9 tells us, "But this happened that we might not rely on ourselves but on God, who raises the dead."

From Paul's perspective, suffering and trials came his way not so he could test his mettle and prove that he had what it takes, but so he would turn his attention away from himself and on to God. Instead of telling himself that he was a strong soldier and that he would get through this if he just gritted his teeth and held on, Paul turned to the One who is so much stronger than him, the One who has the power to raise the dead.

Pastor Mitch Chase again:

> Trials come in all shapes and sizes, but they don't come to show how much we can take or how we have it all together. Overwhelming suffering will come our way because we live in a broken world with broken people. And when it comes, let's be clear ahead of time that we don't have what it takes. God will give us more than we can handle—but not more than he can.[28]

That's the good news in this. And that's the message. When suffering comes your way—and it probably will—it's not up to you to find the strength to handle it. The truth is there is overwhelming suffering and sorrow in this world, far more than any of us would want or be capable of enduring. But God is bigger than any sorrow, and He wants us to rely on Him.

Your suffering might not end in this life. Things might not get better. But if you keep trusting in Him, you will find He gives you the strength to endure whatever comes your way, and that there is an eternal weight of glory waiting for you at the end.

The phrase "God will not give you more than you can handle" is not in the Bible. And it is not something that God has promised us either. The hard truth is that sometimes you will find yourself in circumstances beyond what you can bear.

But God has promised us His strength. He invites us to rely on Him. Stop asking yourself if you are strong enough, and remember that He is.

For further study, see the Discussion Guide for
Chapter 7 on page 144.

– 8 –

EVERYTHING HAPPENS FOR A REASON

I'm That Guy Now

It's happened to me a couple of times recently.

The first time, I was at lunch with a couple of friends. One of them had just received some bad news, so we were commiserating with him. We were listening to the story of what had happened, and talking together about next steps. Basically, we were just trying to be supportive friends. And then, there was a little bit of a lull in the conversation, and my one friend says to the other, "Well, everything happens for a reason."

And immediately—and I'm not real proud of this—I said, "You know that's not in the Bible, right?"

So, I'm that guy now.

I was trying to be funny, but I don't think I came off that way. He knew I was working on this book, so he knew what I was getting at. And, of course, he didn't actually say it came from the Bible. But it did give us a chance to think about whether that phrase is helpful or not.

The second time was a few days later. I was talking to somebody who was in a bad financial situation. He'd been injured a couple of months back. He wasn't able to work, so he wasn't able to pay his bills. He was about two months behind on his rent and utilities. He had applied for disability earlier in the week, and he was pretty sure he was going to qualify, but it was going to take at least a couple of more months for the paperwork to go through. In the meantime, his power was getting shut off and his landlord was getting impatient.

A tough situation. We talked for a while about possible sources of help and different agencies in town. Then, as the conversation ended, he said, "I know everything happens for a reason, I just wish I knew what it was."

This time, I was better. I didn't say anything. But you know what I wanted to say?

Yeah, I wanted to say, "That's not in the Bible." But, more than that, I wanted to say, "It would seem that the reason is that you waited too long to do anything about your problem. You've been behind on your bills for a couple of months, but you only asked for help at the last minute. Now you've made your crisis into someone else's crisis." But I didn't say anything.

"Everything happens for a reason." We've all heard it. We've probably all said it. It's one of the most popular Christianisms out there. And it exists in several forms. When someone is dealing with some bad news, when someone is struggling to make sense of things, we say,

- God must have a plan for all of this.
- When God closes a door, He always opens a window.

- Won't it be great to see how God uses this?
- Isn't it good to know that everything happens for a reason?

If you have ever been on the receiving end of a statement like this, you know how unhelpful it can be.

I was talking with a church small group. Each of us had been through various seasons of bad news. And we agreed that, when you are in the middle of great grief, the last thing you want to hear is that "everything happens for a reason." As one member of the small group put it, "The first person to say it is the first person to be punched in the nose."

Of all the phrases in this book, I'd say this is one of the closest to expressing Biblical truth. We believe that Jesus is the King of the universe. We believe that no matter what happens, He remains in control. Thus, we believe that no matter what happens, God can use it for His purposes, His glory, and our ultimate good. In that sense, there is indeed a reason behind everything that happens.

And yet, the cliché itself, and the way we so often use it, is really not all that helpful. And, as we'll see, it can lead to some ideas that can produce great spiritual harm.

What We Are Really Saying

For this chapter, I'm going to change our questions a little bit. I want to begin by asking: What do we mean when we use this phrase? When we say "everything happens for a reason," what are we really saying?

I believe that when we say "everything happens for a reason," what we are really saying is, "everything (bad) happens for a (good) reason."

We are saying that if a bad thing has happened to somebody, there must be a reason—a good reason—that it is happening.

Which is really only a short step from saying to somebody, "You know, this bad thing that happened to you? It's really a good thing." Or, to use another Christianism, "it's a blessing in disguise."

Right now you're probably thinking, "Russell, that is not what I mean when I say it. What I mean is that God has things under control and that He can take even bad things and use them for good results. I'm definitely not calling a bad thing a good thing." And I totally understand that's not what you're trying to say . . . but it is what's being communicated.

And here's how I know: this is a phrase we only use when we are talking about bad things. You would never dream of using this phrase to talk about a good thing. If somebody comes to you and says, "I got a scholarship to my dream school!" you wouldn't reply, "Well, everything happens for a reason."

You could say that. Getting a scholarship is a part of everything that happens. But if you were to say that in that particular situation, people would think you were a real Debbie Downer. "What do you mean everything happens for a reason? You don't think my scholarship is a good thing?"

We don't use the phrase for good news, we only use it when we are talking about bad news.

So, obviously, we're saying that there is a reason this bad thing happened. And, since we are trying to be encouraging, we're saying that reason must be good. Right? I mean, if your friend totals his truck because he was driving drunk, you can say, "Everything happens for a reason" and what you would mean is that a bad thing happened (totaled truck) because of a bad reason (drinking and driving). But we don't use the phrase that way either. We use it to try to encourage somebody that there must be a good reason for the suffering they are experiencing.

When we say that everything happens for a reason, what we're really saying is that everything (bad) happens for a (good) reason.

And, because we are Christians, that means we are saying that God has caused this bad thing to happen because it fits into His good plan for you. As we say, "It must be part of the plan." Which is to say God has caused this bad thing for good reasons.

Why This Matters

Which leads to our second question: Where is the spiritual harm? We need to think about the implications of this statement. Where does it lead? I have three answers to this question.

1. God-blaming.

As we just saw, saying that everything happens for a reason is pretty much the same as saying that God has caused this bad thing to take place. There can be comfort in that, if you trust that God is good and has your best interests in mind.

But it can just as easily make you bitter and angry at God. "If this is God's plan for me, then I don't like His plan very much! He's not a good God, and I don't like the way He is messing with my life. If everything happens for a reason, then it's God's fault that I'm going through the junk I'm going through, so maybe I'll just be done with God!"

The problem is that we are confusing what God allows with what God causes. God permits things to happen in the world—and to us—and sometimes we assume that He prefers those things. We assume that if God permitted it, then He must have planned it, and therefore He designed these terrible things that have happened to us. But the Bible is clear, in passages like James 1:13 and 1 John 1:5, that God does not cause evil and in Him there is no darkness at all.

So we must stop short of calling God the author of evil. He may have permitted it, but that doesn't mean He caused it. He is able to redeem it, but that's not the same as saying He is to blame for it.

2. Silver-lining searching.

If everything happens for a reason, then—naturally—what do we do? We start looking for the reason. Whenever a dark cloud comes our way, we try to come up with the silver-lining behind it all.

And, frankly, that can lead to some really gross ideas.

Take, for example, a spouse who has an affair. Two marriages are wrecked. Two households disrupted. All kinds of drama and heartache. But maybe the affair leads to a permanent relationship. And maybe that new marriage is really strong and leads to a happy family. "See," the new couple will say, "God has brought us together. It was meant to be."

Seriously?! Do you really think that God wanted you to commit adultery? Do you really think God is in the business of breaking His own commandments to put couples together?

Look, God is all kinds of gracious. He can redeem our worst mistakes, and He can bless families that start out in all sorts of difficult situations. But that doesn't mean our sin is a good thing.

Or, again, maybe you've heard of murderers who have given their lives to Jesus while in prison. "Well," we'll say, "look at the silver-lining. At least something good came out of it. At least this person knows the Lord now."

Really?! Do you really think the only way God could bring that person to salvation was by having him or her kill somebody first? Again, God can overcome sin. He can forgive the vilest of sinners. Even murderers. But don't think for a minute that God designs somebody to be a murder victim just so the killer can come to know Christ.

Searching for the silver-lining can lead us to say all kinds of dumb things. Isaiah 5:20 says, "Woe to those who call evil good and good evil."

Let's be really careful about implying that a diagnosis of cancer, or the death of a child, or a corruption scandal at a major corporation that leaves hundreds of people out of work is somehow a good thing. Because it's not. And if you're ever tempted to tell someone it is, just don't.

3. Misplaced hope.

In his book *10 Dumb Things Smart Christians Believe*, Larry Osborne tells this story:

> I remember the question-and-answer session that followed a talk I gave on "Where's God When All Hell Breaks Loose?" A mother of a severely handicapped young boy stood up. Her son suffered from life-threatening seizures, often occurring daily.
>
> At first she seemed to push back on the idea that God might not be the direct instigator of all that was happening to her son. She claimed it gave her purpose, meaning, and strength to see her son's condition as God's plan for her life.
>
> Then she suddenly started to sob—deep, gut-wrenching sobs. Her next words revealed the dark side of her paradigm: a crushing disillusionment with God. "When will he fix this?" she cried out. "I can't take it anymore. Why doesn't he answer?"
>
> Armed with the conviction that her son's condition was God's doing and would somehow prove to be a good thing in the long run, she was banking on an earthly miracle she would probably never see instead of setting her hope on the eternal inheritance that she and her son were guaranteed to see.
>
> She was caught in an emotional quandary. As long as she saw God as the direct cause of her son's seizures, there was the possibility that he would stop

the seizures. In that, she found great hope. But if he was the direct cause of the seizures, he was also the author of her son's private hell. In that she found great despair.[29]

When we believe that every bad thing happens for a good reason, we start putting our hope in a silver-lining that may never appear. Jesus is our ultimate hope, not the wishful thinking that our suffering will miraculously come to an end.

So…why?

Now allow me to ask another question. Why do bad things happen? If God is not the designer of these bad things, where do they come from?

Obviously, this is a big question, and I could preach on it every Sunday for the next five years and we still wouldn't have it fully figured out. But, in a nutshell, let me give you three reasons bad things happen.

1. We live in a fallen world.

Sometimes bad things happen because we live in a world that is still dealing with the consequences of Adam and Eve's sin. Because of sin, God's good creation has been corrupted and compromised. As it says in Genesis, childbirth became painful and weeds started to grow (Genesis 3:16, 18). As it says in Romans, "creation was subjected to frustration" and is in "bondage to decay" (Romans 8:20–21).

It's because we live in a fallen world that nervous systems sometimes go haywire and little boys are subjected to near-fatal and oft-repeated seizures. It's because we live in a fallen world that healthy cells within our bodies mutate and go from being helpful servants to our well-being to cancerous traitors that threaten our very lives. It's because we live in a fallen world that sharks attack, horses stampede, and bears rip up campers' tents.

More than that, it's because our world is fallen that many of the laws of nature that we count on to be helpful and predictable can also work against us and cause great damage. For example, the gravity that keeps us from flying right off the surface of this planet also means a plane that loses power will crash to the ground. The same low-pressure system that brings much needed rain to the crops of the Midwest can first exist as a hurricane in the Gulf of Mexico that will devastate the coast. The same immune system that protects us from bacteria and viruses can also attack our bodies in the form of autoimmune diseases like rheumatoid arthritis or multiple sclerosis.

Simply put: Bad things happen because our world is broken.

2. We deal with fallen people.

Sometimes bad things happen because the people around us are sinful and some of the sins they commit directly impact us.

If everyone descended from Adam is infected with sin, then everyone you meet is a sinner. Sin is a universal condition. And that means some of the bad things people do are going to cause problems for other people.

Make a list of the worst things that people can do to each other: racial discrimination, sexual harassment, rape, child abuse, trafficking, murder, mass shootings—those bad things happen, not because God has a good reason, but because sinful people are committing sin.

And it's not just the really, really bad things and the really, really bad people. Your friends and family are sinners also, and many of their sins are going to hurt you. That means sometimes your friend will betray you, sometimes your boss will lie to you, sometimes your spouse will lose his or her temper and say an unkind thing. Those are bad things too, and they happen because we live in a fallen world with fallen people.

But, those aren't the only reasons bad things happen.

3. We have a fallen nature.

The bad isn't just out there, it's also inside of us. Let's face it. A lot of the bad things that happen to us are the result of choices we have made.

Not all of those choices are necessarily sinful, some are just foolish. Maybe we didn't think a decision all the way through, maybe we didn't do enough research. But if you make a bad investment and your portfolio is wiped out, if you fail to look both ways and drive into oncoming traffic, if you wear socks with sandals and ruin your social standing, those choices have consequences. It's silly to blame God for our bad choices.

Moreover, a lot of bad things happen to us because we do make sinful choices. If you fail out of school because you didn't go to class and you didn't do your homework, don't say that God must have had a good reason for letting it happen. If you are in jail because you've been writing bad checks and skipping out on your creditors, don't ask why God is making you go through this. Sometimes the chickens come home to roost.

The world is fallen. Other people are fallen. We are fallen. In a world like that, bad things are going to happen.

The God of Purpose

I believe strongly in God's control and governance of our world. Some theological terms that are important to me are *God's sovereignty* and *providence*. That means I do not believe in things like fate, or luck, or chance. I do not believe that things happen in the world that are ever beyond God's supervision or control. Some Bible verses which express these ideas are Isaiah 46:9–10:

> Remember the former things, those of long ago;
>> I am God, and there is no other;
>> I am God, and there is none like me.
> I make known the end from the beginning,
>> from ancient times, what is still to come.
> I say, "My purpose will stand,
>> and I will do all that I please."

God does all that He pleases. I take that to mean that nothing can happen outside of His will. Or, as Proverbs 16:4 says: "The Lord works out everything to its proper end—even the wicked for a day of disaster."

God is guiding things where He wants them to go.

The way I often explain this is I do not believe that God can be surprised. I do not believe there has ever been a thing in my life—a good thing or a bad thing or anything in between—where God has looked down from heaven and said, "I can't believe that happened to Russell!" or "I did not see that coming."

For me, if that were possible, I'm not sure God would even fit my definition of what it means to be God. That is to say, if there are things happening in our world that God is not strong enough to see coming or powerful enough to stop, then He's really not much of a god at all.

I know that raises a bunch of questions. I know it sounds like I'm talking out of both sides of my mouth. On the one hand, I'm saying that God does not plan or design the bad things that happen to us, while on the other hand I'm saying that nothing happens that God does not know about in advance or could not stop if He decided to.

This can be very confusing. We're dealing with some of the mystery of what it means to be God. But both of these ideas are taught in scripture, and I believe both are true.

As I mentioned earlier, it is sometimes helpful to think about what God permits and what God plans. He does not directly plan all the evil in the world, but He does permit it. And He's not surprised by it. And, most importantly, He's not defeated by it.

Which leads me to Romans 8:28. This is the verse that probably gets cited the most often when we talk about the phrase "everything happens for a reason." It's the verse that seems to teach that very idea: "And we know that in all things God works for the good of those who love him, who have been called according to his purpose."

This is a great promise, one of the most precious promises in scripture. It's a verse to treasure, and a verse to cling to in the midst of hard times.

But let's think about what this verse is not saying. For one thing, this is not a promise for everyone. The promise here is specifically for those who love God and have been called according to His purposes. That leaves out a lot of people, and a lot of things that happen.

For another thing, this verse is not saying that everything that happens is good. Or even that everything happens for a good reason. It is promising that in all things God is at work for the good of His people (those who love Him and have been called). Osborne writes:

> In other words, even the enemy's best shot can't thwart God's ultimate plan. God can and will accomplish his good purposes no matter what. But that's a far cry from saying that everything that happens is somehow good or necessary.[30]

The point is that nothing happens to those who love God that is beyond His ability to restore, renew, and redeem. The beauty–and the promise–of Romans 8:28 are not that every bad thing that happens to us will eventually prove to be a good thing, but that, no matter how bad things get, God's ultimate and eternal purposes for us—our ultimate good—will not be foiled.

The Redeeming Power of the Cross

I first preached on this cliché and the problems with it several years ago. The conclusion of my sermon focused on those three words: Restore. Renew. Redeem. I urged the congregation to resist the desire to uncover the reason behind all their trials, but rather to trust in God's ability to restore, renew and redeem even the worst things that happen to them.

More recently, some bad things happened to me. In the midst of my trial, I received a card in the mail from a college student who had been in the congregation for that sermon. She wrote,

> I am not going to say "everything happens for a reason." I still remember that sermon from three years ago. The words "Restore. Renew. Redeem." are written inside the cover of my Bible from that sermon. I know God will restore, renew, and redeem this situation.

In the midst of my grief, it was jolting to hear my words spoken back to me. Instead of trying to find a good reason for the bad that had occurred in my life, I was led instead to find hope in God's ability to renew and restore.

As Christians, we don't believe that every bad thing has a good reason behind it, but we do believe that our good God can redeem the bad for His good purposes.

God does not design anyone to be a murderer or a molester, but even the worst of sinners are not beyond the reach of His forgiveness. God does not ordain broken families, but even out of brokenness He can bring wholeness and restoration. God does not cancel out the consequences of the fall, but in spite of our fallenness He keeps working for our redemption.

And the way that works is through the cross of Jesus Christ. Here's the very worst of all the worst things that could happen: The Son of God put to death by the human beings He created. And yet it is this tragedy that God uses to absorb all the sinfulness and brokenness and fallenness of the world. God can work all things for our good through the filter of Christ's death and resurrection.

We don't get promised a reason for everything that happens to us, but through the cross of Jesus, we do get the promise that everything—including us—can be redeemed.

For further study, see the Discussion Guide for
Chapter 8 on page 147.

Conclusion
DO NOT SETTLE FOR EASY ANSWERS

Reticular Activating System

A few years ago, I bought a Dodge Avenger. It is a fairly nonde-script, mid-size sedan that has served me well. Five stars. Would buy again.

Prior to buying the car, I had only the vaguest sense that such a thing as a Dodge Avenger existed. I knew about Dodge, of course, but I'm not sure I would have been able to identify an Avenger out of a line-up of other Dodge products.

After buying the car, however, I began seeing Avengers every-where. I'd notice them at stoplights and in car lots and waiting in line at the school drop-off: "Look kids, a car just like Dad's!" Perhaps you have had similar experiences. It's sometimes called the "red car phenomenon." Buy a red car and suddenly you are overwhelmed by how many other red cars are on the road.

Scientists say it has something to do with our Reticular Activating System (RAS). The RAS is a bundle of nerves located in our brainstems that filters out unnecessary information so that our brains can focus on the important stuff. It is the RAS that allows new parents to sleep through the sound of a passenger jet roaring overhead and yet snap instantly awake at the sound of the baby crying. It is the RAS which allows us to focus on the story our dinner companion is telling even while we are surrounded by the noises of a crowded restaurant.

Scientists also believe the RAS is the reason we learn a new word and then start hearing it everywhere. They believe that once a concept or idea has been brought to our conscious mind, the RAS begins to let it through the filter more often. That's why it seems like everyone has purchased the same model car as you did.

Something similar has happened to me since beginning work on this book. Once I started thinking about Christian clichés, it seems like I notice them all the time. Not just the ones I wrote about, either.

More and more I find myself hearing people make short and declarative statements as though they were definitive truth, and I am questioning just how true those statements are.

I hope this book will do something similar for you. Not that you will become the obnoxious person who says, "You know that's not in the Bible, don't you?" whenever one of these phrases is uttered. Instead, I hope:

- You will be attentive and critical of all the information you receive.
- You will not settle for simplistic answers or tired clichés when contemplating the great mysteries of life.
- You will be like the Bereans and examine the scriptures to see if what you are being told is true.

Keep Asking

To that end, let me encourage you to be a person who continues to ask questions. Maybe not out loud, but in your mind at least. When you hear a pithy statement uttered as declarative truth, or a slogan proclaimed as though it should be the end of all further discussion, don't be afraid to think it through. Use these questions that guided us throughout this book to think critically and Biblically about the information you receive.

Is there any Biblical truth?
Is the statement an actual Bible verse? If it is, has it been quoted accurately? Does the use of the statement line up with the Biblical context?

If it is not a verse in the Bible, does the main assertion of the idea line up with other Biblical truths you are familiar with? Can you discern which Biblical truth that the statement is attempting to convey?

Where does the statement go wrong?
Is this phrase more of an expression of secular thinking or Biblical thinking? What popular and worldly wisdom might the statement be derived from?

In what ways is the phrase dismissive or callous of the circumstances others are experiencing? How has the effort to be pithy made the idea of this phrase seem trite?

What other Biblical truths or realities does the idea ignore?

Is there better news in the gospel?
How can the great truths of salvation by grace, God's sovereignty, and our compassionate care for one another be brought to bear in this situation?

What Bible verses and stories can bring hope even if there are no easy answers?

Digging Deep

When Jesus tells the parable of the wise and foolish builders, He specifically says that it is a story about hearing His words and putting them into practice.

The foolish builders choose a poor foundation. They skip the hard work of digging down to bedrock and erect their house directly on the sand. We might say these are people who settle for familiar clichés and easy answers. They are people whose faith is built on slogans and catchphrases. But Jesus warns that when the storms and floods that are the trials of life come to these people, their faith will collapse like a sandcastle.

But the wise builders choose a better foundation. They do the hard work of digging down deep so that their house can be anchored to rock. We might say these are people who ask questions and examine the scriptures. These are people whose faith is built on learning and practicing the truths of the Bible, whether they are easy or hard. And Jesus says that when the storms of life come to these people, their faith will remain firm. (See Matthew 7:24–27 and Luke 6:46–49.)

As Christian clichés begin to pop out at you like red cars in a parking lot, I pray that you will not settle for the shifting sands of catchy slogans, but will have the firm foundation to evaluate them Biblically and critically.

Think it through. Ask questions. Don't settle for easy answers. And build your life on the solid rock of Jesus' gospel.

ENDNOTES

Chapter 1

[1] "God helps those who help themselves" (December 1, 2021) In *Wikipedia* https://en.wikipedia.org/w/index.php?title=God_helps_those_who_help_themselves&oldid=1058055870

[2] Adam Hamilton, *Half-Truths: God Helps Those Who Help Themselves and Other Things the Bible Doesn't Say* (Nashville: Abingdon Press, 2016) 69.

Chapter 2

[3] Mercedes Streeter, "Woman Crashes Into Multiple Cars And A House At 120 MPH After Letting 'God Take The Wheel'," Jalopnik.com July, 19, 2021. https://jalopnik.com/woman-crashes-into-multiple-cars-and-a-house-at-120-mph-1847319454 (Accessed December, 29, 2021)

[4] Danielle Johnson and David Chang, "Death of Faith-Healing Couple's Son Ruled a Homicide," NBCPhiladelphia.com. May 21, 2013 updated May 22, 2013. https://www.nbcphiladelphia.com/news/local/death-of-faith-healing-couples-son-ruled-a-homicide/1956560/ (Accessed November 16, 2021)

[5] Madison Park, "Parents clash with state, kids in medical decisions," CNN.com. May 27, 2009. https://www.cnn.com/2009/HEALTH/05/27/parents.medical.custody/index.html (Accessed January 4, 2022)

[6] Larry Burkett, *The Complete Financial Guide for Young Couples*, (Colorado Springs: David C. Cook, 1989) p. 87.

[7] John Piper, "Are You a Passive Christian?" [Video Series]. *Look at the Book*. February 9, 2017. DesiringGod.org. https://www.desiringgod.org/labs/are-you-a-passive-christian

[8] J.I. Packer, [@JIPacker_] "Tweet Message." *Twitter*. August 16, 2010. https://twitter.com/jipacker_/status/21339299962?lang=en

Chapter 3

[9] Ken Myers, "The Pursuit of Happiness," *Ligonier.org*, September 1, 2008. https://www.ligonier.org/learn/articles/pursuit-happiness (accessed November 5, 2021)

[10] ... "Ruth Graham: World Tired of Plastic Christians," Christian-post.com, Nov. 6, 2008. https://www.christianpost.com/news/ruth-graham-world-tired-of-plastic-christians.html

[11] Santos, Laurie. (Host). You Can Change (No.1) [Audio podcast episode]. T*he Happiness Lab*. Sept. 12, 2019. Pushkin. https://www.hap-pinesslab.fm/season-1-episodes/you-can-change-w6YOz

Chapter 4

[12] Don Pierson, "Jan. 5, 1993: Mike Ditka loses his job with the Bears, but not his passion," Chicago Tribune, January 5, 2018 https://www.chicagotribune.com/sports/bears/ct-mike-ditka-fired-bears-1993-20180105-story.html (Accessed January 5, 2021)

[13] Rose Fitzgerald Kennedy, "Quotable Quote," *Goodreads.com* https://www.goodreads.com/quotes/659138-it-has-been-said-that-time-heals-all-wounds-i (accessed Nov. 5, 2021)

[14] Worth Kilcrease, "Time Heals All Wounds, Or Does it?," *Psychology-Today.com*, April 24 2008. https://www.psychologytoday.com/us/blog/the-journey-ahead/200804/time-heals-all-wounds-or-does-it (accessed Nov. 5, 2021)

[15] Allison James, "Does Time Heal All Wounds?," *griefrecov-erymethod.com*. March 19, 2015. https://www.griefrecoverymethod.com/blog/2015/03/does-time-heal-all-wounds (accessed Nov. 5, 2021)

[16] Kilcrease, "Time Heals."

17 Billy Graham, "10 Quotes from Billy Graham About Grief," *Billygra-hamlibrary.org* September 6, 2019. https://billygrahamlibrary.org/blog-10-quotes-from-billy-graham-on-grief/ (accessed Nov. 5, 2021)

18 Chris Witts, "Does Time Heal All Wounds?" *hope1031.com.au* March 4, 2019. https://hope1032.com.au/stories/faith/2019/time-heal-wounds/ (accessed Nov. 5, 2021)

19 Victoria Strong, "Time Does Not Heal All Wounds?" *Huffpost.com* April 24, 2016. Updated December 6, 2017 https://www.huffpost.com/entry/time-does-not-heal-all-wounds_b_9732158 (accessed Nov. 5, 2021)

20 Ibid.

21 Ibid.

Chapter 5

22 Information taken from Bill Quigley and Amer Rmanauskas, "Seven Places Where Haiti's Earthquake Money Did and Did Not Go" Haitilib-erte.com. January 27, 2015. http://haiti-liberte.com/archives/volume5-25/Seven%20Places.asp (Accessed November 5, 2021) and Jonathan M. Katz, "Disaster Aid: How US charity begins at home." *Theguardian.com*. January 11, 2013. https://www.theguardian.com/books/2013/jan/11/haiti-us-charity-begins-at-home (Accessed November 5, 2021)

23 David Mathis, "Generosity Begins at Home," DesiringGod.org. March 2, 2015. https://www.desiringgod.org/articles/generosity-begins-at-home (Accessed November 5, 2021)

24 Randy Alcorn, *Money, Possessions, and Eternity: Revised and Updated Edition*, (Carol Stream, IL: Tyndale House, 2003) 391.

Chapter 6

25 Jon Bloom, "Don't Follow Your Heart," DesiringGod.com. March 8, 2015. https://www.desiringgod.org/articles/dont-follow-your-heart Jack Sparrow's compass is a reference to the movie *Pirates of the Caribbean*.

The character, played by Johnny Depp, has a compass that does not point to True North but rather, points "to the thing you desire most in the world."

[26] Ibid.

Chapter 7

[27] The quote and the moving analogy come from Mitch Chase, "God Will Give You More Than You Can Handle," Thegospelcoalition.org, July 17, 2015. https://www.thegospelcoalition.org/article/god-will-give-you-more-than-you-can-handle/ (accessed November 10, 2021)

[28] Ibid.

Chapter 8

[29] Larry Osborne, *10 Dumb Things Smart Christians Believe*, (Colorado Springs: Multnomah, 2009) 98.

[30] Ibid.

DISCUSSION GUIDE

The following questions are provided for you to dive deeper into these phrases by yourself or with a partner or small group. Discussion of these clichés will also help equip you to spot other Christianisms and evaluate them Biblically. Along those lines, the discussion guides are arranged around our three key questions:

- Is there any Biblical truth?
- Where does the statement go wrong?
- Is there better news in the gospel?

In addition to the chapters in this book, brief videos have been prepared to help everyone in your group come to the discussion with the material fresh in their minds. These videos can be accessed for free at:

www.EatThisWord.com/Misquoted

DISCUSSION GUIDE - CHAPTER 1
GOD HELPS THOSE WHO HELP THEMSELVES

Opening Discussion:

1. In what sort of situations have you encountered the phrase "God helps those who help themselves?" Prior to reading chapter 1, was your opinion of this phrase favorable or unfavorable? How would you have explained its meaning to someone who was unfamiliar with it?

Watch the chapter 1 video: www.EatThisWord.com/Misquoted.

Is there any Biblical truth?

2. This cliché has its origins in the fables of Ancient Greece and Benjamin Franklin's *Poor Richard's Almanac*. What do these beginnings tell us about the meaning of the phrase?

Read 2 Thessalonians 3:10–12 and Proverbs 10:4.

3. How can a person who is not working be disruptive to God's community?

4. How does the Biblical teaching about personal responsibility compare to the ethic of "God helps those who help themselves?"

Where does the statement go wrong?
5. What are some examples from your own experience or situations you are familiar with where the phrase "God helps those who help themselves" has been used to justify questionable behavior?

Read Deuteronomy 15:7–8 and James 1:27.

6. Why do you think God so frequently calls on His people to be generous toward the poor and distressed? How does giving to those in need help to authenticate our faith?

7. In what ways does the Biblical call to be "open-handed" toward the poor undercut the teaching of "God helps those who help themselves"?

Is there better news in the gospel?
Read Psalm 10:14, 17–18.

8. What does the Bible say about those God loves to help? What other scriptures come to mind?

Read Romans 5:6–8.

9. How does the self-help ethic of "God helps those who help themselves" run counter to the gospel message of salvation by grace?

Evaluation:
10. On a scale of 1 to 10, where would you rate the phrase "God helps those who help themselves?"

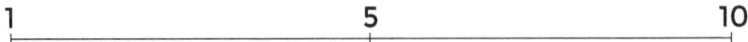

1   5   10

1 = this phrase should be stricken from all Christian usage

10 = this phrase may not be in the Bible, but it conveys important truth

DISCUSSION GUIDE - CHAPTER 2

LET GO AND LET GOD

Opening Discussion:

1. In what sort of situations have you encountered the phrase "Let go and let God?" Prior to reading chapter 2, was your opinion of this phrase favorable or unfavorable? How would you have explained its meaning to someone who was unfamiliar with it?

Watch the chapter 2 video: www.EatThisWord.com/Misquoted.

Is there any Biblical truth?
Read Matthew 6:25–34 and 1 Peter 5:7.

2. List some of the reasons Jesus tells us not to worry about food or clothes.

3. Ultimately, Jesus points to God's care for us as motivation to release our anxieties to Him. How does this capture the message of the phrase "Let go and let God?"

Where does the statement go wrong?
4. Russell says that the logic of "Let go and let God" can be taken to some very dark places. What are some examples where Christians have ignored ordinary means of help in the expectation of extraordinary intervention by God?

Read Psalm 91.

5. Make a list of some of the remarkable promises in this Psalm?

6. How do you reconcile these promises with the reality that sincere followers of Jesus still experience sickness and death?

7. How does the story of Jesus' temptation (where Satan quotes Psalm 91 as a reason for Jesus to jump off the temple) caution us against reckless risks of faith? (See Matthew 4:6–7.)

Is there better news in the gospel?
8. How does Jesus' example of God feeding the birds (Matthew 6:26) illustrate the difference between faith and presumption?

Read 1 Peter 5:7–9 and Philippians 2:12–13.

9. Explain how these verses assert human effort alongside trust in God. How can confidence in God spur us on to greater efforts in following Him?

Evaluation:
10. On a scale of 1 to 10, where would you rate the phrase "Let go and let God?"

1	5	10

1 = this phrase should be stricken from all Christian usage

10 = this phrase may not be in the Bible, but it conveys important truth

DISCUSSION GUIDE - CHAPTER 3

GOD JUST WANTS ME TO BE HAPPY

Opening Discussion:

1. In what sort of situations have you encountered the phrase "God just wants me to be happy?" Prior to reading chapter 3, was your opinion of this phrase favorable or unfavorable? How would you have explained its meaning to someone who was unfamiliar with it?

Watch the chapter 3 video: www.EatThisWord.com/Misquoted.

Is there any Biblical truth?

2. What would you say to someone who views God as opposed to happiness and fun? What indications does the Bible give that God wants us to experience good things in life?

Read Psalm 1:1–3.

3. How does the word "blessed" show that God is not opposed to happiness?

4. How does Psalm 1:2 put limits on the "whatever makes you happy" mindset?

Where does the statement go wrong?

5. In what ways has the pursuit of happiness come to define our culture?

6. Russell diagnoses three problems that come when we start to believe that God's highest priority for us is our happiness. What are they? How do they run counter to scripture?

Read Hebrews 11:24–26.

7. In what ways did Moses' status as a Prince of Egypt give him access to worldly happiness?

8. How does Moses' choice illustrate some things the Bible considers more important than short-term happiness? (Consider John 14:23–24 as well.)

Is there better news in the gospel?
9. Describe the difference between happiness and joy. How can the pursuit of joy be more sustainable in the long term than the pursuit of happiness?

Evaluation:
10. On a scale of 1 to 10, where would you rate the phrase "God just wants me to be happy?"

| 1 | 5 | 10 |

1 = this phrase should be stricken from all Christian usage

10 = this phrase may not be in the Bible, but it conveys important truth

DISCUSSION GUIDE - CHAPTER 4

TIME HEALS ALL WOUNDS

Opening Discussion:

1. In what sort of situations have you encountered the phrase "Time heals all wounds?" Prior to reading chapter 4, was your opinion of this phrase favorable or unfavorable? How would you have explained its meaning to someone who was unfamiliar with it?

Watch the chapter 4 video: www.EatThisWord.com/Misquoted.

Is there any Biblical truth?

2. Why do you think the use of clichés is so prevalent when talking with someone dealing with grief?

3. For many physical wounds, the passage of time brings healing. Why is that a tempting analogy for emotional wounds? In what ways does the analogy fall short?

Read Psalm 31:15 and Psalm 90:12.

4. What do these verses teach us about God's relationship to time and our attitude towards it?

Where does the statement go wrong?

5. Russell uses the analogy of a flat tire to illustrate that the passage of time cannot fix every problem. Can you think of other examples of problems that do not repair themselves?

6. What do these examples say about the need to actively engage in a grief recovery process?

Is there better news in the gospel?

Read Isaiah 61:1–2 and Isaiah 53:3–5.

7. What do these verses say about Jesus' mission on earth as it relates to our grief and suffering?

8. What does it mean to call Jesus the "Wounded Healer"? How does knowledge of Jesus' earthly suffering encourage us when we turn to Him in the midst of our own sorrow?

9. How is the advice given by Victoria Strong at the end of this chapter helpful for engaging with those who have suffered loss?

Evaluation:

10. On a scale of 1 to 10, where would you rate the phrase "Time heals all wounds?"

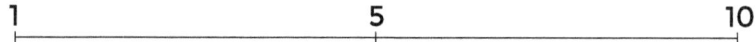

1   5   10

1 = this phrase should be stricken from all Christian usage

10 = this phrase may not be in the Bible, but it conveys important truth

DISCUSSION GUIDE - CHAPTER 5

CHARITY BEGINS AT HOME

Opening Discussion:

1. In what sort of situations have you encountered the phrase "Charity begins at home?" Prior to reading chapter 5, was your opinion of this phrase favorable or unfavorable? How would you have explained its meaning to someone who was unfamiliar with it?

Watch the chapter 5 video: www.EatThisWord.com/Misquoted.

Is there any Biblical truth?
Read 1 Timothy 5:3–8.

2. When this passage talks about widows who are "really in need," what does it mean?

3. How is the person who refuses to provide for the members of his or her immediate family failing to live up to even the minimum standards of Christian practice?

Where does the statement go wrong?
Read Philippians 2:3–4.

4. How do we sometimes use the phrase "Charity begins at home" to justify selfish behavior?

5. Why is it dangerous to treat compassion like a finite resource?

6. How does a "leftovers" mindset lead us to be less generous?

Is there better news in the gospel?
Read 2 Corinthians 8:9 and Matthew 25:37–40.

7. How is Jesus the ultimate example of unselfishness?

8. In your own words, make the Biblical case for why Christ-followers should be sacrificial in their giving.

9. Russell suggests that when this phrase was first coined it meant something like "Charity is learned at home." How does that change your understanding of this cliché? How does that align with the Biblical call to generosity?

Evaluation:

10. On a scale of 1 to 10, where would you rate the phrase "Charity begins at home?"

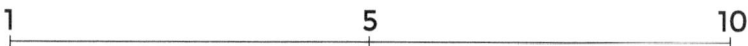

1 = this phrase should be stricken from all Christian usage

10 = this phrase may not be in the Bible, but it conveys important truth

DISCUSSION GUIDE - CHAPTER 6

JUST FOLLOW YOUR HEART

Opening Discussion:

1. In what sort of situations have you encountered the phrase "Just follow your heart?" Prior to reading chapter 6, was your opinion of this phrase favorable or unfavorable? How would you have explained its meaning to someone who was unfamiliar with it?

Watch the chapter 6 video: www.EatThisWord.com/Misquoted.

Is there any Biblical truth?

Read Psalm 37:4.

2. The second line of this verse sounds a lot like the cliché "Just follow your heart." How does the context (including verse 3) show that this is not a blanket promise for God to give us whatever our hearts desire?

3. What does the line "delight yourself in the LORD" tell us about what our hearts should desire most? (Consider Romans 12:1–2.)

Where does the statement go wrong?
Read Jeremiah 17:9 and Isaiah 6:5.

4. The advice to "just follow your heart" presupposes that our hearts will always lead us on the right path. Give some reasons that supposition is not accurate.

5. In what ways can cultural norms desensitize us to bad ideas? Give some examples.

Read 1 Corinthians 4:3–4.

6. How does Paul display humility concerning what his own conscience is telling him?

7. How does the Biblical teaching that it is the Lord who judges us work against the popular usage of the phrase "Only God can judge me?"

Is there better news in the gospel?
Read Romans 6:17–18 and Colossians 3:1–2.

8. How does the miracle of salvation overcome the deceitfulness of our hearts?

9. As Christians, what can we do to train our hearts to desire the right things?

Evaluation:
10. On a scale of 1 to 10, where would you rate the phrase "Just follow your heart?"

1   5   10

1 = this phrase should be stricken from all Christian usage

10 = this phrase may not be in the Bible, but it conveys important truth

DISCUSSION GUIDE - CHAPTER 7

GOD WILL NOT GIVE YOU MORE THAN YOU CAN HANDLE

Opening Discussion:

1. In what sort of situations have you encountered the phrase "God will not give you more than you can handle?" Prior to reading chapter 7, was your opinion of this phrase favorable or unfavorable? How would you have explained its meaning to someone who was unfamiliar with it?

Watch the chapter 7 video: www.EatThisWord.com/Misquoted.

Is there any Biblical truth?

Read 1 Corinthians 10:13.

2. How does the background information about Corinth as a place of idol worship and sexual immorality inform our understanding of this verse?

3. What does this verse teach about our relationship to old patterns of sin once we have become followers of Christ?

4. The cliché "God will not give you more than you can handle" is often applied to situations where we are suffering or enduring difficult circumstances. How does that application go beyond what Paul is saying in this verse?

Where does the statement go wrong?
5. We like to think that God hands out trials in a "fair" manner. Give some Biblical examples that would suggest this is not the case.

6. Russell suggests that the phrase "God gives His hardest battles to His strongest soldiers" is ultimately a discouraging idea. Why?

Is there better news in the gospel?
Read 2 Corinthians 1:8–9.

7. What phrases in these verses indicate that Paul felt he was in a situation beyond what he could handle?

8. How does God use difficult circumstances in our life to grow us in our relationship with Him?

9. Why is relying on God's strength better news than relying on ourselves?

Evaluation:

10. On a scale of 1 to 10, where would you rate the phrase "God will not give you more than you can handle?"

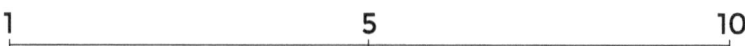

1 = this phrase should be stricken from all Christian usage

10 = this phrase may not be in the Bible, but it conveys important truth

DISCUSSION GUIDE - CHAPTER 8

EVERYTHING HAPPENS FOR A REASON

Opening Discussion:

1. In what sort of situations have you encountered the phrase "Everything happens for a reason?" Prior to reading chapter 8, was your opinion of this phrase favorable or unfavorable? How would you have explained its meaning to someone who was unfamiliar with it?

Watch the chapter 8 video: www.EatThisWord.com/Misquoted.

Is there any Biblical truth?

2. Russell says that when we say "Everything happens for a reason," what we really mean is "Everything (bad) happens for a (good) reason." Do you agree or disagree? Why?

3. How does belief in the sovereignty of God lead us to believe God must have a design for every bad thing that happens? How do you

support belief in God's sovereignty without assigning Him blame for every tragedy?

Where does the statement go wrong?
Read Isaiah 5:20.

4. How does the search for a silver-lining lead us to imply that bad things are actually good?

5. How does the search for a silver-lining lead us to put our hope in promises that may never appear?

Is there better news in the gospel?
Read Romans 8:20–23.

6. How does the doctrine of the fall help explain the existence of suffering?

7. According to Romans 8, who or what has been affected by the fall?

Read Romans 8:28.

8. How is saying that God "works for the good" different from saying that everything that happens is good or has a good reason?

9. Russell finds great hope in the words, "Restore. Renew. Redeem." What do these words mean to you? How can they bring comfort in the midst of suffering?

Evaluation:
10. On a scale of 1 to 10, where would you rate the phrase "Everything happens for a reason?"

1	5	10

1 = this phrase should be stricken from all Christian usage

10 = this phrase may not be in the Bible, but it conveys important truth

ACKNOWLEDGEMENTS

A big "thank you" to Pastor Matt Mitchell who served as the first reader and had a lot of helpful advice. Also, thanks to Pastors Mike Brost and Steve Petroelje who have been great friends and steady rocks in the midst of a storm.

Thanks to all those who participated in the Monday Night "Misquoted" Bible Study in the Loft. It was a lot of fun, and your support means more than you can know.

Thanks to Nathan, Bryan, Eric and Jason. You are my team, and it is a joy to count you as friends. Thanks to all who have supported Eat This Word Ministries with your prayers and gifts.

Thank you to Rhonda Fleming of Anchoring Hope Publishing for editing this work and helping to get it out to the public. You are so easy to work with! And finally, thank you to Joana Franca for being my assistant and coming up with the concept for the cover art.

www.ingramcontent.com/pod-product-compliance
Lightning Source LLC
Chambersburg PA
CBHW060532130626
46553CB00002B/718